T0301185

Half-Arse Human

Also by Leena Norms

Bargain Bin Rom-Com

Half-Arse Human

How to live better without
burning out

Leena Norms

JOHN MURRAY

First published in Great Britain in 2024 by John Murray (Publishers)

3

Copyright © Leena Norms 2024

The right of Leena Norms to be identified as the Author of the Work has been asserted by her in accordance with the Copyright, Designs and Patents Act 1988.

Illustrations © Leena Norms

A CIP catalogue record for this title is available from the British Library

Hardback ISBN 9781399820295
ebook ISBN 9781399820318

Typeset in Fournier MT by Palimpsest Book Production Limited, Falkirk, Stirlingshire

Printed and bound in Great Britain by Clays Ltd, Elcograf S.p.A.

John Murray policy is to use papers that are natural, renewable and recyclable products and made from wood grown in sustainable forests. The logging and manufacturing processes are expected to conform to the environmental regulations of the country of origin.

Carmelite House
50 Victoria Embankment
London EC4Y 0DZ

www.johnmurraypress.co.uk

John Murray Press, part of Hodder & Stoughton Limited
An Hachette UK company

The authorised representative in the EEA is Hachette Ireland, 8 Castlecourt Centre, Dublin 15, D15 XTP3, Ireland (email: info@hbgi.ie) *for The Gumption Club*

Contents

Half-Arse Manifesto

—

RECYCLING THE RULE BOOK

Hello, my name is Leena and I am a half-arser.

In the past I would **never** have owned up to being someone who half-arses things.

If you were a 'half-arser', you were:

Insincere, flaky, disingenuous, sloppy, lazy.

Who would want to be any of those things? Being a half-arser, in my mind, was the opposite of everything I wanted to be: passionate, driven, successful, intentional.

I wanted to be, for want of a better phrase, *a whole-arser.*

There's a whole section in every bookshop promising that it's possible, if I'll only follow their 'simple' steps. A miracle morning, killer career, healthy relationship, harmonious calendar and immaculate house are all just a few page-turns away; all I need to give is 110 per cent of my life source. Everything I've got.

1

Slight problem: I'm usually already running on half a tank. The tank is low. I'm rummaging through the pockets of my soul and turning out my energy reserves only to shake out loose change and moths (how did— never mind).

What they want me to give simply isn't there for the giving. While I've always picked up my pen, my toothbrush, my keys and my fork with the best of intentions, I've often found myself passive when I've wanted to be passionate. Drudging, when the plan was to be driven. The road to success, as it turns out, is filled with booby traps and quicksand and lined with hecklers who shout 'you're doing it wrong!' before you've rounded the first corner.

So, I'm ashamed to say, I sat it out. Very little 'arsing' was done. I stewed in the guilt like an ogre in a swamp, I blew bubbles, I tried to relax.

At least, I thought to myself, *I'm not a hypocrite. I won't try until I know I can commit. I'm just 'not in that place right now'.*

I could take pride in knowing that I had spared the world my half-arsed attempt. That would have been insulting. Insincere. Cringe.

THE RESURRECTION OF THE HALF-ARSER

Where did my aversion to half-arsing come from? What am I picturing that is so awful?

If we're thinking literally, 'half-arse' alludes to only being half on our seat throughout life. We only ever have one cheek down, ready to run away, never fully committing to the show. Or perhaps it's not as bad as that. Perhaps we're on the *edge* of our seat; we're so immersed in what is happening elsewhere, we lean forward trying to catch every word, and in the meantime forget to enjoy the full experience of SITTING. Sure, we're not making full use of the seat, but at least we're making contact.

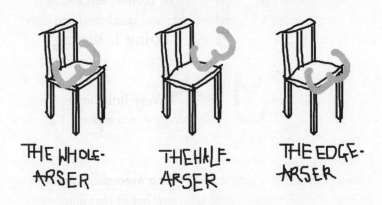

THE WHOLE-ARSER   THE HALF-ARSER   THE EDGE-ARSER

The problem is, while we're looking at all of these arses, judging which technique might be best, we're doing something much worse.

We're hovering.

The hovering arse is the position before the half-arse. Someone whose arse is forever in a liminal space between walking away and hunkering down for the ride. They fear the hypocrisy of the half-arse or the shame of picking the wrong chair. Some people hover for years. I call it *the squat of death*.

This space is where hope goes to die.

you.

If the diagram above is you, you're an arsehole.
Bear with me here; I mean that in the most affectionate way
possible. There is a specific kind of emptiness that comes
with *knowing* what needs doing, or what you really want, and
feeling helpless to make it happen. Pile that on top of the
guilt you've been stacking against yourself for years ('I am
too privileged/lucky/loved/spoiled to be feeling this way!')
and you're probably ready to topple over. There's a hole
where your plan should be, and I have a suspicion it's not
your fault.

When we give up on starting, we're not only potentially
screwing over other people; people in our house, people in
our communities, people who we'll never meet. We're being
an arsehole to ourselves.

4

Sounds like you? Ready to stop hovering and start a whole-arsing adventure?

Unfortunately, I can't get you there. This is not a book about being successful in life. It's a big ask and, frankly, I've given up.

I've accepted that I'm never going to have boundless energy, or perfect timing, or suspiciously good luck. Life is full of recessions and surprise illnesses and those 2 a.m. phone calls that change everything. Planning an upwards trajectory in a world where the tectonic plates of economy, influence and technology are constantly shifting beneath our feet is a fool's errand. I can't have been the only one to have had that revelation over the past few years. Yours might have happened when you were watching an election result, or wiping down your food shop, or watching a record-breaking rain cloud descend on your town. The world is weird, and it's about to get weirder.

There are, however, specific projects and people I would like to go 'all in' on. While there's so much I have no control over, I know that there are parts of the world I *must* be able to improve. Somehow. I bet you have some too. This is a book about stripping back your expectations, making peace with *not* doing everything – while also refusing to be someone who does nothing. It's a journey into what is *actually* worth your time, and what can simply be half-arsed. There might be more than you think.

I've realised (just in time) that the world is made up of strategic half-arsers. They've given up on the 'thinking with the head versus heart' dichotomy and opted to simply think with their arse and get done what they can. Not only are they changing the world; they're having a proper laugh along the way.

THE FOUR TYPES OF ARSEHOLE

If there's a hole in your arsing, we can fill it. Here's some tell-tale signs it's time to half-arse things . . .

YOU'VE STOPPED BELIEVING YOU'RE CAPABLE OF ANY ARSE AT ALL

The crash diet has a precedent we all recognise: you overhaul your eating habits to the extreme, keep it up for a little bit and then spectacularly quit, swing into over-eating, feel bad about yourself and then begin the whole wretched cycle again. I think that crash dieting has a cousin: crash self-improvement. You might have mainlined one too many self-help books or podcasts, and (because they were too extreme or pushed advice that didn't fit your reality) spectacularly failed to obey their tenets. You might have felt as though it is you who is the problem. That you are simply 'out of arse', that you can't do anything right. It's not that you don't care, it's that you're just oh so very tired. What little energy you have can't be enough to be useful. Can it?

YOU'RE IN A FREEZE RESPONSE

You're acutely aware that there is SO much to be arsed about in the world: there are a million skills to master, views to ogle at, careers to conquer . . . besides that, there's so much to fix: laws to change, trophies to seize, ceilings to break. Then there are all the things to perfect: your beliefs, your butt, your book collection, your stance on beef, your beauty routine, your breakfast bowl.

The enormity of it all makes your brain fizz . . . and then flatten. You're not numb to the brazen wonder of it all; your inaction comes from a place of feeling overwhelmed. You're frozen by the idea that you might choose the wrong destination, the wrong person to love, the wrong thing to fix about yourself or the world. Haunted by the fear of missing out, you decide that it would only be *fair* to miss it *all*.

YOU HAVE MORE AMBITION THAN CAPACITY

You get a real rush from a resolution hastily made – you hear what you *could* have, or achieve, or be and you're headfirst down the lane towards it before anyone can shout 'magic beans!' Trouble is, you only have two legs and one space-time-continuum, so as the resolutions stack up, so do the discarded fingernails. It turns out that you can't bite your way back to balance. The plates pile, the deadlines fly by and, more often than not, you're left with a few mismatched pieces of puzzle that are less than the sum of their parts. You're a failure, a fallen talent, a privileged piece of mush on the shoe of your generation. Or, at least, that's what it feels like. Everyone thinks you're smashing it, but secretly *you* know you're arsing it up.

Even when you're spinning plates with a smile, you're always one sneeze away from falling arse-over-tit.

YOU'RE HALF-ARSING ALL WRONG

You are muddling through on autopilot. You feel like you 'should' be making an effort, or setting ambitious resolutions, but you're already arsing up the *small* things you try to change. You've spent so much energy de-coding the food aisle to work out all the ways to shop your way out of being 'The Worst Person Ever' (Palm Oil? Avocados? Is free-range even *that* free?). You've bought the online course for 'the thing' you want to be good at, but you've never even opened it. You have huffed your furniture round your 'spacious' living room in four different calibrations, but it still looks more passé than Pinterest. You don't have any more brain real estate to spend on the things you desperately want to improve, so you're starting to think it's the end of the road for you and transformation. This is just the way you are.

Any of these resonate? Which one of these arseholes are you? Perhaps you're a mixture of two or all four. How suave! You're almost a cocktail, so give yourself a delicious name. I'm the Breakdown Bramble. Now we've diagnosed the problem(s), let's start sniffing out a solution.

AN INTRODUCTION TO HALF-ARSE MATHS

I'm the first to say that I am not a maths whizz. My brother coached me through passing GCSE maths in exchange for me doing his art homework. He's almost three years younger than me.

Despite a rocky start, I've learned to make maths an unlikely accomplice in times of confusion. In this instance, I think some simple charts might help us tell our arseholes from our elbows.

The Dunning–Kruger Effect, which is a cognitive bias in which people with limited competence in a particular domain routinely overestimate their abilities, was first described in 1999 by two social psychologists (Justin Kruger and David Dunning), and was the result of the research they conducted to discover the real dynamics between confidence and competence. Since their findings, numerous studies have been conducted on novices and experts, in fields as diverse as chess, medicine, politics, business, aviation, sports and literacy, all in a quest to understand the gap between self-assessment (how good we think we are) and objective performance (how good we actually are).

These show how, in those early stages, when you first learn a skill but aren't yet good enough to really assess your own work, your confidence skyrockets. Then, as you start to really understand what makes a good piece of work, your assessment of your progress becomes more accurate: you're still improving at the same rate, but the contrast in how you felt about your work at the beginning and how you feel now makes your confidence plummet.

If you can push through that perfectionism, and accept the reality of where you're at, the joy of the end of the x-axis awaits you! If you decide in the middle of the graph that your current 'best' is just not good enough, you're more likely to down tools and stomp off. To me, it was a real lightbulb moment that shed some light on why so many people get stuck at the beginning of a process and can't accurately assess where they're at, largely leading to them giving up . . . JUST before they start making real progress.

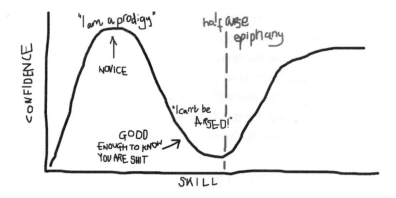

By applying the Dunning–Kruger principles to elements of our lives beyond our main skillset or profession, we can see where we might be going wrong.

What if we applied it to everything we think we're failing at: the decoration of our home, our lack of political action, our understanding of our own spirituality?

Throwing ourselves into 'finding our personal style' in one shopping trip, or giving up ALL animal products overnight, can *feel* amazing in the short term, but won't keep our bums on the seat as the x-axis progresses and the weeks wear on.

Our obsession with personal narratives doesn't help, I'd wager. We want to be able to tell a simple transformation story, sometimes subconsciously trying to tidy it before we even begin changing ourselves. Satisfying titles our brain loves include:

The day I quit _____
The one hack that changed my _____ *habits*
The moment I realised _____

Whether we're planning to share our transformation on social media, or just anticipating relaying it to our friends and family, story matters. We're the hero, and we have been transformed. The 'before' and 'after' is so clean cut, that the person we were 'before' can't be confused with the person we become after. We don't need to answer for the 'before' person's behaviour. We're absolved of our guilt. We're not them. We're a *new us*.

There's no transformation story more alluring than the new year's resolution. To explain why I'm a resolution-sceptic, more maths is needed, I think . . .

BERT VERSUS ERNIE

Bert and Ernie, hungover on Ernie's sofa on January the first, both watch a hard-hitting documentary and are inspired to cut down on their meat and dairy consumption. They both decide to put a marble in a jar for each vegan meal they manage to eat that month.

Bert signs up for Veganuary, orders a t-shirt, and starts practising his 'deprived but it's worth it' sad face for when the cheesy chips round is ordered at the pub. He tells *everyone*. He even sticks to it.

Ernie has a wedding in a few weeks, and he sent his meat-loving dietary requirements form to the bride and groom *months* ago. He's also off to visit his dementia-haunted nan to celebrate his birthday, and since his grandad died, he's always been the one to help her cook one of the only meals she still remembers how to make him: honey-roast ham. He can't imagine telling her he won't eat it. He also lives in a more rural spot than hot-shot city-slicker Bert. The only sandwiches stocked within a fifty-mile radius are strictly mayo-based and proudly meaty. He can try to plan, but he's got a stressful day job and he knows he's slow to form new habits. He decides to do what he can.

Here are their jars on the first of February:

BERT   ERNIE

There's a clear winner, right? Bert cackles, demands a round at the pub for winning, and then celebrates by lounging with his favourite Meat Feast pizza on the sofa, where it all began.

Ernie however, keeps filling his jar. He acquires a taste for jackfruit. By March he's started ordering his coffees with oat milk. In May he finds a pub in his village that does a mean nut roast. He still has a big steak on his birthday and a

Nutella pancake when he's on holiday, but he's started cutting out all the animal products he was never really that bothered about in the first place. He still has the occasional Curly Wurly, his absolute favourite chocolate bar, a swirling ladder of caramel-decked deliciousness. He doesn't take himself too seriously, his eye is off the ball *often*. He is a half-arser.

Here are their jars on 31 December:

BERT   ERNIE

Your brain, like Bert's, might have been trained to think in absolutes: for thousands of people Veganuary has been the gateway to a plant-based habit that's lasted a lifetime. But you don't have to do a perfect, flawless Veganuary to beat Bert at his own game. (More on this in our chapter on being a half-arse vegan.) My point is, I imagine the piglets don't care which one of the boys called themselves 'vegetarian'. The oceans don't breathe a sigh of relief every time someone shares a 'fish are friends not food' infographic on Instagram. The methane levels in the atmosphere don't fall every time someone uses the #veganuary hashtag.

They fall meal by meal.

THE UNEXPECTED JOYS OF HALF-ARSING IT

By the end of this book, you will be perfect.

Just kidding – but I'm also kind of serious. We'll go through all your mental drawers and give everything a good going over; give your pongy opinions of yourself a wash and inspect what your 'perfect' actually looks like. We'll look at your ambitions, your houseplants, your skincare routine (or lack thereof). We'll hold up your life goals to the light and check they don't have holes in them. We'll waft your career ideals in the air and give them a good sniff, we'll poke around your fridge and your wardrobe and your wallet. And after all that spring cleaning, we'll write *your* true, accurate definition of 'perfect', then lay the foundations of how to make it happen.

And on the way you might just pick up some extra, unexpected joys . . .

INTENTIONAL HALF-ARSING IS A CONFIDENCE SHORT-CUT

I often look back at the times when I wasn't arsing at all, and am amazed at how much brain space it took up to

NOT do something. While I was busy telling myself I didn't have time to make an imperfect start, I was using an untold amount of EXTRA energy fretting about not beginning. I'd go over my various shortfallings, daydream about how far I would have come by now if I'd only started years ago, spend hours absentmindedly weighing up the pros and cons of starting . . . *soon*. Any day now.

The psychologist Viktor E. Frankl often discusses in his research the effects of mental anguish: how it shrinks your inner life, often distracting you with primitive wishes and thoughts (where can I get my next binge, treat, hit?) and pushes you into using apathy as a coping mechanism.

I used to think that it would cause me *anguish* to attempt something and do it wrong; that by hovering over the seat, I was protecting myself from distress. What I've realised is that by planning to half-arse something and following through on my more realistic goals, I'm building credibility with myself, where before there was only scepticism. By *halving* my expectations and then meeting them, I'm building an internal track record that I can pull out and wave in my own face, should I doubt my ability to commit to bigger goals in the future.

Your honour, I object: Leena has in fact flossed TWICE this week, meeting her half-arse goal. It cannot be said that she is a COMPLETE arse.

Even if we're struggling with our identity as a 'good' person or a 'hard worker', half-arsing sets aside identity. For a moment, it invites you to put your self-hatred on ice and become a 'doing' over a 'being' for a little while. It's not about who you are. You – for now – are a verb, not a noun. Don't think about whether you can change yourself; that's a big task and might not even be necessary. It's much less daunting to make a plan about how you might *do* something, based on what your *current* resources are. Putting half-arse plans in place gives you a lower bar to meet, which is especially useful for anyone with a deep sense of self-hatred. There's a bigger leap than you'd think between 'I can't do it', and 'I *can* do it, but I will probably arse it up a bit'. When we make a plan, we're showing that we're capable of making a plan, and judging when something is done *enough*. We're appointing ourselves worthy of judging which parts of the job are most important, and which parts we can miss out. If we don't trust our performance, we can at least be a great project manager of our own inadequacies.

It's one thing to whisper 'I can do it! I am amazing!' into a mirror. It's quite another, more powerful, project to build yourself a case for self-belief. I want a body of evidence, however small, to bring before the jury of myself. I want to vote in my own favour, and I want to mean it.

HALF-ARSING HELPS YOU SEE WHERE THE CRACKS ARE

If you haven't started something (whether that's eating vegan, improving your home, or clearing your inbox) it's very hard to predict what the friction points in that project might be. You can take a wild guess, but the practical mysteries of completing a task often like to lurk in the shadows and only emerge once you've actually begun.

That task might be trying to clear your diary to do just one hour every week of creative messing about – exposing how absurdly chock-a-block your diary is with non-essential things that, you realise, now you think about it, you agreed to do on autopilot. It might be the fury of realising, once you try to spend more time outside, how few green spaces there are in your area. It might be saving up and donating to a charity that is doing good work, only to find out your workplace invests your pension in people who are trying to do the exact opposite.

Trying to achieve change on a personal level can often highlight the outside forces that deter you from *even* half-arsing it. It's infuriating but it's necessary; half-arsing it also halves the resentment and leaves some energy for a more effective wrestle with what is really stopping you.

I always joke that I'm not altruistic, I'm just quietly furious. I'm only half-joking: I now spend as much time trying to reimagine the structures that hold us back from getting everything done as I do wondering why I can't get everything done. That's got to be progress, right?

Your arse doesn't exist in a vacuum, and once you work out that *you* are not the *whole* problem, you might need that other half of your energy reserves to plan some productive system-changing high jinks.

HALF-ARSING GIVES YOU A DIRECTION

We're clearing your brainspace for a reason. We're clearing it so you can go 'whole-arse' on the important

things OR go 'soularse searching' for what is really
important to you.

If you already know what you want your focus to be, it's a
really good 'North Arse' (forget North Stars! In self-help
circles this is known as 'knowing your *why*', but I personally
think 'finding your North Arse' is much more
inspiring), because this helps alleviate the guilt around half-
arsing in other areas.

There might be some of you who are still looking for a
focus, who might read a chapter where I suggest half-arsing
something and find that you completely disagree with my
advice. The thought of half-arsing that subject sounds
wrong, or sad, or like you'd be missing out.

GREAT! You might have found your North Arse.

Alternatively, you might start half-arse and realise which part
of the system needs fixing, and start itching to give it a real,
whole-arse go.

Who knows, by the end of this book, you might have
become flammable enough to let the world light a fire under
your arse again!

HALF-ARSING MAKES YOU NICER

Not only can half-arsing give you more time, a little
perspective, and make you calmer, it can also help you
understand other arseholes better. Once you have admitted
to yourself that demanding 100 per cent in every area of

your life is unrealistic, you start to be a little more peaceful when other people fall short, too. The dangerous myth of being someone who 'gives everything their all' can quickly poison our relationships with other people. Once we start openly, vocally half-arsing various parts of our life, and being able to explain why ('I don't think that matters to me as much as I thought it did'/'I don't think that high bar is realistic'/'I'm only able to give this much because I'm focusing on this'), it leaves space for other people to be honest about what their real priorities are, and where you fit in.

BECAUSE THE FLOOR IS MADE OF LAVA

'The Floor is Lava' was one of my favourite games growing up: a rainy-day battle between us and our parents' furniture. The challenge was to get from one side of the room (or, if you're playing on expert mode, the house) without touching the floor. You'd hover on windowsills, perch on the backs of armchairs, swing from curtains, or even travel by space hopper – the only rule was that you couldn't touch the floor because, obviously, it was made of lava. Our parents' floral carpet transformed into a frothing fire of dark magma, gurgling up from the depths. If you fell in, it was mandatory to make a pantomime of dying a gruesome, guzzling death; mouth frothing and limb-waving encouraged. It's a perfect cocktail of grim peril and physical humour and, honestly, I have no idea why I ever stopped playing it.

The phrase popped back into my head when I swallowed my fear and cracked open my first book about the climate crisis. There were graphs that made me go cross-eyed and predictions that made The Purge look cheerful. I'd heard so many of these terms before, made fluffy in my mind through repetition and indifference: The Planet, Our World, The Environment.

I had subconsciously been processing this 'thing' as something separate to myself – something 'out there' to save if I had time, when I got around to it. A disaster that sounded unfortunate, but not entirely my problem. Only really urgent to those who like hikes or get overly sentimental about birds.

But that wasn't it at all.

The researchers were talking about the floor. The musty, floral-filled, weird-smelling carpet of life on which everything else was built. Matted with dog hair, splattered with tea, strewn with toys and old magazines – the only floor we've got. However good we are at balancing on furniture, if it goes, sooner or later we go with it.

So, I'm going to give a little scream here, a tiny one, not at you, just to release a little pressure valve in my heart before we can continue. Join in if you need to.

THE FLOOOOOOOOOR IS MAAAADEEE OF LAVAAAA!!!!!

Okay, all better.

You might be thinking:

'Bloody hell, woman. There's no need for that, I'm just looking for some tips on how to organise my socks and get a bit more done.' or 'Hang on, I didn't sign up for a book about green stuff!'

I'm afraid what I'm hearing is:

'I didn't expect to pick up a book that mentions the floor!'

This book isn't an attempt to transform you into an activist. I'm not one myself. BUT I do think that we can be more effective in our personal lives – and our political lives, should we choose to become active – if we stop trying to get everything right. If we stop thinking that we either 'save the world' ourselves or 'stay out of it', as if there aren't a million options in between. If we stop being surprised when the people around us do the same. And so, since the floor is lava, there has never been a better time to give half-arsing a go.

By the end of our time together I hope you'll have an action plan on how to clear your desk of all the stuff that has been clogging up your to-improve list. Half-arsing is not a pathetic half-attempt at success. It's not admitting failure before you've even begun. It's not a cop-out. It's a strategic form of optimisation you build for yourself, based on the reality you know about you, and the floor you live on. It's perhaps the most optimistic thing you can do in a beautiful and sticky and crumbling world. It's a cop-in, a promise that you're in it for the long haul.

A pact with yourself, and the floor, and the other Floor People, that it's not over. The arsing about has just begun.

In some ways this is a book about limits – the limits of ourselves, our time, our world.

But it's also about expanding – lovingly prodding and rolling out what we have like dough, testing what happens if we pull it apart, mess with it, add some sprinkles.

It's also a book about verbs, how we *become* what we do. As long as we take it slow. Very gradually, before our very eyes, the most apathetic of arseholes can put their bum on their seat, rev the engine and disappear into an adventurous dawn.

I've watched lives unravel and re-plait themselves into shapes so beautiful it would make your eyes water. I've read about towns and countries that have become kinder, gentler, stronger over time. There's no radical star player, no hero who led the pack, no tangible moment when 'it all changed'. Just thousands of people, in snatched moments, muddling along, throwing what they can at the wall, trusting that some of it will stick.

It's a story arc that would make a rubbish Hollywood film plot.

It also happens to be the recipe for a really top-notch life.

Now turn the page and say it with me:

Anything worth doing is worth half-arsing.

Half-Arse Choices

Before we start sorting our arses from our arse-nots,
we have to check our ammo. It's important that we're
sure of our ability to choose to half-arse and stick to it,
but also of our strategies for making choices in general.
Each chapter in this book will require us to trim off
parts of our to-do and to-be lists, and you'll need a
head for choices to fully embody the intentional
half-arse life. So, let's look at how we make decisions.
Not only in order to forge a way forward, but to
shed some light on how we got into this mess in the
first place . . .

Most catchphrases about making choices *sound* cheerful. The
thing is, they are also truly awful advice.

TRUST THE PROCESS!
(What does that even mean? What if your process is the
whole problem?)

NO REGRETS!
(I think we've all met people who could do with having a
few more regrets)

THERE IS NO DECISION THAT CAN'T BE UNDONE!
(This applies only to time travellers and wizards)

YOU ARE YOUR CHOICES!
(For all of our sakes, I hope not)

And my least favourite:
JUST GO WITH WHAT FEELS RIGHT!
(As if any of us can really *know* how we're feeling at any given moment. Most of the time I can't even tell whether I'm hungry or just bored. Anyone who doles out the 'feels right' advice has never had hormones, or lived in a country with WEATHER and presumably always has a good night's sleep. Or, more likely, is lying.)

Feelings or no feelings, it turns out that adults *have* to make decisions, and often pretty important ones. We rarely have the luxury of time, infinite wisdom or help; they just have to be made.

The hardest lesson in life for me was not 'HOW TO MAKE THE PERFECT DECISION EVERY TIME, NO ERRORS', but learning that *deciding* to decide is half the battle. I'm a procrastinator extraordinaire, and if there's a decision to be waylaid, I will waylay it. Without fail, this has always resulted in *either* making the decision harder, or someone else making the decision for me. The chance to make the decision passes and even if I *would* have skipped the opportunity anyway, I end up lumped with regret because I didn't intentionally *choose* to pass it up. I learned the hard way that avoiding making a hard decision can ruin your life faster than making a bad but manageable one.

There's a reason films like *About Time*, *Jumanji*, *13 Going on 30* and *Groundhog Day* are so appealing: who wouldn't find life a lot easier if we knew that we could backpedal after making the wrong choice?!

Making choices is objectively **terrifying** if, like most people, you're not an all-knowing being with a flawless sense of self and complete confidence in what you want.

In my opinion, the words 'every decision is permanent' should only be said aloud when accompanied by a strong shot of tequila and followed up with a comforting Curly Wurly. But, shot or no shot, the statement is still true.

Every decision is permanent, and with permanence comes the risk of *shudders* . . . *regret*.

WHAT TATTOOS TAUGHT ME ABOUT REGRET

The first tattoo I ever got was in Reno, Nevada. I'd been volunteering with a conservation group, building trails in the desert in the day and sleeping under the stars with a rag-tag band of Americans at night. It seemed that everyone in the crew except me had tattoos, and around the campfire and on long hikes I became known as the person who would (I hope respectfully) ask them to tell me the stories behind them; like where they got them, or how long ago. In my defence, one of the boys had a tattoo of Osama bin Laden hugging an alien: however prim and unintrusive you aspire to be, the sight of that would test anyone's propriety.

I heard stories of loss, of fierce protection, of whimsy. Of wild nights out and days spent indoors with the curtains closed. One of my indigenous friends traced the meaning of a sleeve that stretched from her collarbone to her wrist: echoes of her ancestors wound around her arm like arteries. Another wiggled her shoulder to animate the rainbow cockerel that protected her heart from all the dark and dank things she had realised it needed protection from. Then it was my turn.

'What tattoos do you have?'

They'd all assumed mine were hidden, that I'd pull up my shirt and return the favour with a heartfelt tattoo story of my own.

'Oh – I'm . . . I'm not really a tattoo person.'

A murmur of confusion passed through the group. I guess, for a 'not-a-tattoo-person', I sure was nosey about people's tattoos.

That night I let what I'd said echo around my head. *Not a tattoo person.* I was nineteen and didn't spend much time dwelling on 'my youth'; most of my energy was focused on feeling as old and grown up and put-together as possible. In that moment, I decided I might be being a bit of a knob.

Wasn't it a bit early to be making statements like 'I'm not *this* kind of person, I'm not *that* kind of person'?

What kind of *anything* was I?

In every human culture on record, people have been poking themselves with sticks and jamming some ink under their skin with the expressed intent of leaving it there, for ever. Getting tattoos is far from a new phenomenon: everyone from Neolithic icemen to ancient Britons have been at it for thousands of years. It's brought the bearers everything from solace to belonging, comfort to self-expression; and presumably, just like me, the majority of our ancestors thought they looked pretty cool.

So, why had I been so scared of them? Why were so many other people?

Fifteen years on, and six tattoos later, I've received enough anxious questions about my tattoos from family, strangers and the man at my local computer repair shop to be able to sort the themes of their concerns into three main categories:

Does it hurt?

Will you be able to get a job?

What will you do when you get old?

These worries aren't unique to tattoos. They're such raw anxieties and say so much about what terrifies us all, deep down. We can extrapolate these fears into any potentially permanent decision we make. The triple threat fears that are always there:

- the fear of pain
- the fear of scarcity
- the fear of aging

After all, you can't undo the effects of pain on the mind and body; once you've lost access to resources it's very hard to recover them; and once you get old there's no way to turn back time.

If you're making the decision whether or not to have children you might think: what if it's painful to push something the size of a watermelon out of something the size of a lemon? What if it's painful to love something that much? What if I can't provide for them? What if I don't have enough to offer them emotionally? What if I age before it's even possible? Or, if you end up deciding not to have children: what if it is painful *later*, if I regret not having them? What if I don't have enough people in my life and I'm lonely? What if I grow old and there is no one to look after me?

Perhaps you're deciding whether to quit a job: what if my boss/colleague/partner is angry at me for leaving? What if my next job isn't as fulfilling or doesn't pay as well and I can't go back? What if I screw up my financial future and can't look after myself in old age? Or: what if I stay miserable in this current role? What if I become stagnant in my career and this was my one chance to get out? What if I regret not quitting when I'm older and this opportunity never comes up again?

There's spooky, permanent consequences wherever you turn. The world is a spooky place. The key is to be the brave one in the haunted house, to keep making choices, to stay in the real world. To make a decision is to refuse to fade; to not let the world make a ghost out of you.

Want to hear something else scary?

hands you a shot Every decision is, on some level, permanent.

Of course, some bad choices can be recovered from, rectifiable in time; but even the 'reversible' ones are never truly reversible, since we can never truly retrace our steps and regain the time we lost taking a wrong turn.

If we can accept that, and that the risk of regret is *literally always on the table* whatever we do, we can stop feeling stressed by the very existence of a decision that's facing us and just get on with making it. I did end up getting a tattoo in Reno. Not because I thought I would always love it, or because I thought I might be able to reverse or remove it in the future. I got it to remind me that it's okay to make decisions with the desires, tastes and information you have on hand at the time. That I should trust my future self to laugh, forgive and deal with younger-me's choices. That all choices stick, so I might as well get used to it, and that I shouldn't ring-fence who I am before I've even tested the waters.

Permanence and mark-making on the body haven't always scared us. Tattoos haven't always been a sign of rebellion or something that could lead to ostracisation. Quite the opposite. They've been a way to say: I belong here, I commit to this, I want to join in on the choosing, because choosing is what makes us human. I like the sound of being human. *Now poke me with that spiky thing!*

Ready to make one of those pesky decision things? Step right this way.

WAYS TO MAKE A DECISION WITHOUT HAVING A MELTDOWN

I realise that giving you a choice of ways to solve a problem about choices could be slightly counterintuitive. In my defence, you don't really need to choose between these methods. If one in particular doesn't stick out to you, why not try them all? Abundance mindset! I've arranged them in an order that goes from 'dip a toe in' to 'complete disaster prevention', so feel free to work through them chronologically and see what sticks.

PRO/CON WITH PIZAZZ

If you've never made a pros/cons list about a breakup, have you even been living? It would shock you if you heard the kinds of weighty life decisions I've chalked up to the 'for and against' approach. Preferably on real paper, written with the aid of a big mug of hot chocolate. Not only does it feel more real to get it down in ink, but it also makes it untraceable, and completely destroyable. Why is that important? Because the first ingredient in my recipe for a perfect half-arsed pros/cons list is brutal honesty.

In the digital hellscape of shared devices and open screens, you *will* self-censor, even if subconsciously. Because the slightest possibility that your manager could read 'sharing a desk with her is like sharing a hammock with Elon Musk', or 'I have seen road accidents more cheerful than her response to my presentation' will skew the results, so if taking to old-fashioned pen and paper that you vow to burn afterwards helps, do it.

The second ingredient is a **weighted ranking.** As a humanities graduate, I am loath to admit that, yet again, *maths might be the answer*, but here we are. Not all pros are created equal, and if they're treated as such, you might come to a conclusion that will ON PAPER bring euphoria into your life, but in practice make you miserable. For example, if you were deciding on whether to attend a far-away wedding:

perfect excuse to wear that sequin dress I have no business owning otherwise and am plagued by guilt about having bought

. . . might score a two out of five for importance. Whereas:

the bride is actually my childhood bully and I would rather drink battery acid than see her happy

. . . might deserve a slightly higher ranking. Five for importance, let's say.

Or, here's a [censored] version of a pros/cons list I made when deciding whether it would be a good idea to move away from the lovely but expensive capital city I'd spent my twenties living in:

LONDON PROS

Great job opportunities (3)
Friends are here (4)
Great public transport so never
have to pass my driving test (5)
Don't have to travel for
gigs/shows (2)
Living where 'everything is
happening' (2)
Good vegan food (3)

LONDON CONS

Constantly worried about getting
evicted/rent rise (5)
Might mean I never own a place
of my own (5)
Everything takes an hour to get
to (4)
See less of family/childhood
friends (4)
Life is frantic (3)
Soot in my nose (2)

If you know what the pros/cons are, but aren't sure how to rank them, it's great to crowdsource the wisdom of a few friends you trust. Their job is to interrogate how true each entry on the list is and how important it is to you.

'Do you really need to live in London to get the job opportunities you want? Are they definitely the ones you want? Have you thoroughly checked out whether they exist elsewhere?'

'What parts of it make you feel frantic? Can you find a way to stay and feel less frantic?'

'Can't you just blow your nose?'

Once you feel like you have accurate rankings for each pro and con, simply do a tally and let the numbers decide!

FLOWCHARTS FOR THE FRAZZLED BRAIN

Sometimes, when there's a decision on the line, the 'what if'/'what next' of it all slowly starts to burn the wiring in my brain and it becomes impossible to think straight.

There was a period in my life a few years ago, caused by a little-known global pandemic, that meant that my partner Craig and I were very much between lives. We'd moved from London into temporary accommodation in Derby, away from our families and most of our friends, with no idea what to do next.

Craig was working on a temporary remote contract for a job he didn't want to stay in. I'd recently gone freelance in an online economy that seemed, at best, fickle. We didn't really know where in the whole country we wanted to live next, only that we couldn't afford to go back where we came from. To make matters more surreal, it was illegal to have guests over and I was in the phase of lockdown where I was still wiping down our food shop with baby wipes for fear of germs. In an ideal world we'd have loved to be able to internalise the advice of 'live in the moment', 'what's for you won't pass you', 'trust the process'. But if you'd offered those phrases to me at the time I probably would have said something along the lines of:

'I don't trust the process as far as I can throw her, she's a slippery bitch. If you see her, tell her to hurry the fuck up!'

So, as serenity didn't seem like an option, we leaned into the 'what if'. You see, the 'what if', in corporate office speak, is roughly translated as 'flowchart'. Credit to Craig, it was him who came up with the idea of drawing an elaborate flowchart of possible events every time our situation changed. We stuck it to our fridge, and every time I said a variation of 'are we going to be okay?'/'what's going to happen to us?'/'what are we going to do?', he would give me a hug and silently point at the chart.

The flowchart flowed with us in response to what changed in our thought processes and circumstances. I ripped it up and re-drew it several times a week and took great comfort in inspecting it before bed. Of course, I didn't know which one of the bubbles I'd end up in, but I'd carefully made peace with each one. Five dead certainties is *nowhere near* as good as one, but it's astronomically better than none.

If you're stuck in a decision freeze, I highly recommend taking the time to make a big flowchart of all of the possible ways that situation could play out. You might have an ideal route, but if that falls through, at least you know vaguely what your next move will be. Perhaps you can draw a variety of different routes to the same outcome. That way, a single decision doesn't feel as loaded. And it means you can, perhaps, lead a life where you're only HALF worrying about the future, and HALF getting to arse around.

If you can't trust the process, at least you can watch it unfold across your fridge.

DELAYED RATIFICATION

Yes, you read that right. We're here to ratify, not gratify. This option still involves making a decision, but with a twist.

You know that feeling when someone offers you a choice between two pieces of cake; it's only once you've picked one and watch as the other enters their mouth that you realise you made the wrong choice. You really wanted *that* flavour, *that* shape, *that* size slice. I'm sure there's a word for this psychological phenomenon, but I'm going to call it 'picker's regret'. In other words, *don't it always seem to go that you don't know what you've got till it's gone?* I could have as easily called this the 'Big Yellow Taxi' method, but I didn't want to age this book, or myself.

Instead of trying to escape this phenomenon, I try to use it as a superpower. I look at the decision and ask myself: when does this decision REALLY need to be made? When do I need to communicate my decision to someone else, or start a process? Can I MAKE the decision today, but stall acting on it for a little while? Delay the 'ratification', the final sealing of the deal, even if it's just for a few hours or days?

I name that timeframe, and then I make the decision. Immediately.

The next bit requires a bit of Theatre Kid energy, but don't worry; even if you've never harnessed it before, I really think there's a little dramatic self-delusion in every one of us.

Play pretend with yourself that that decision is permanent. Believe it. Sit with it. Live with it. Wash the dishes, have a shower, get on with your day as if it's a closed case. After a few hours, a day, a week, how do you feel?

If you feel relief, indifference or just a little bit of peace; great! Activate that decision! Send the text, book the train, bleach those eyebrows!

However, if you've got that sinking 'I should have chosen the other bit of cake' feeling . . . phew! Also: great news. You've snatched DATA from the jaws of despair (more on data collection in the next method) and you can return to the drawing board with a new set of eyes. No harm done. We have defied the laws of permanence, using only our own powers of self-deception.

Okay, since we're already in drama mode, let's set a scene to demonstrate the practical applications of this madness:

After hours of deliberation, I decide I'm turning down a party invite. I tell myself that while it would be fun, I'm too busy, I'm too tired, it's too far to travel. It's an agonising decision, but I keep going round in circles and I'm sick of my own thoughts. So, for all intents and purposes, to me, in my internal reality, it's not happening. I won't go.

So, I should probably RSVP, right?

Wrong! Instead, I set an alarm/a reminder/even schedule a message for the next day, to RSVP turning it down. Then I live my life like I've already said no. Usually, within a few hours, I'll feel totally at peace about it (or even have forgotten all about the party), OR I'll feel disappointed. Gutted that I'm missing out on seeing friends, or getting to dress up, or started dreading the night in that I know I'll squander on scrolling.

In that case, even though all my hesitations still stand, I know that I really truly *want* to go. The inconveniences are obviously worth it to me. I RSVP yes and know that I've made something *resembling* a good decision.

BAD CHOICES AS DATA COLLECTION

If your choice hasn't been made yet because you feel like you don't have enough information to make the decision, is there a way to make the decision to optimise for information-gathering, rather than instant happiness?

For example, if you were to say to me: 'I'm not sure whether to book a holiday with my boyfriend; he wants to get planning, but we've been going through a rough patch.'

I would suggest that you go ahead and book the holiday. But, instead of treating it as a pressured 'perfect' getaway for which you'll have to patch up your problems and be ready to take cute couple photos in front of monuments whose names you can't pronounce, reframe it as an information-gathering exercise. Sounds like a great opportunity to rejig your communication in a new context. Write a list of questions/concerns you have about the relationship, and promise yourself that you'll either talk about them with your partner or observe your dynamic while away and answer them for yourself. Schedule a lone-coffee-date check-in with yourself for when you return, and be honest about your findings.

Or you might say, 'Leena, I don't know whether to quit my job. I've been offered a job that's completely different and I've got no way of knowing for sure whether it will make me happier or if I'll miss the familiarity of what I have now.'

I'd probably say GO FOR IT; with the caveat of being really mindful about how you frame the decision with yourself, privately. Sometimes there isn't a way to know what will work for you without trying it for a long period of time first. Going into the job with the expectation that it will be better (then, if it's not, either sitting in denial and being miserable or festering in shame for making the wrong decision) is a recipe for regret. Say 'yes' with the simple expectation that it will be *different*, and that you're there to *collect data about yourself*, not to be instantly happier.

There are often ways to tell yourself you've made a decision, while knowing, in your heart-of-hearts, that whatever you've chosen doesn't commit you to a choice long term; that you won't 'lose face' with yourself if you want to retract it, because that was always the plan. The plan wasn't to make a permanent decision, but to collect some decision data.

Sometimes a decision needs to be made, even when the facts and figures are lacking. That's okay. When you reframe yourself as a detective, rather than a nervous wreck teetering on the edge of a precipice, not only can you get closer to an answer, but you have a perfect excuse to wear tweed.

WRITE TWO LETTERS

Accept that you don't have all the information you need, but before you make your decision, write two letters to your future self. If a whole letter seems like sentimental overkill, the message can be the length of a short text.

If you're really extra (as I am) you can schedule them to be emailed to you on a date in the far future when you imagine you will have the full picture about whether the decision was a net positive for your life or not.

When I was deciding whether to write this book, I scheduled the following two emails to myself:

Dear Leena,

So the book was a flop, huh? How many kitchen-floor-resets have you had so far? I don't know if it was the writing that cracked you, or the promotion, or maybe (eek) the ghastly online reviews. In all fairness, it was a long shot, but you have always *loved* a long shot and your life has been built on the few fab harebrained schemes you've managed to pull off. So how were you supposed to know this one was a doozy? It really *did* seem like a good idea at the time. And remember that you asked *lots* of people's opinions who you trusted too, so it wasn't just you who looked at the facts and thought 'this could work!' I still think we'd have been a total toad not to try and I hope you can forgive our audacity. Please don't let this kill your love of a long shot, past-you would be gutted to know you gave up writing because of one shrivelled balloon.

Leena x

Hi Leena,

Thanks for taking some time out of your busy schedule to read an email from a NOBODY. I hear you're a BIG SOMEONE now, I can't believe they liked it! I can't believe you pulled it off! No offence but I can't believe you even FINISHED it. Hope you're having a big gin on me.

Don't get too big for your boots, you were a 'someone' all along, and probably still a little bit of a dick ;)

Leena x

It seems silly because *it is silly*. The letters written in your own defence aren't really for your future self, but to help your present one. You're releasing yourself from potentially feeling guilty about ruining your future self's chances, and trusting that an older, wiser you (even with just a few more days under their belt) will give 'present you' a break. You've even made sure to remind yourself that you did the best you could, with the information you had. I bet 'future you' will give you grace.

STILL CAN'T DECIDE?

If you've given these methods a go and you're still none the wiser as to how to approach a particular decision, it could be that you're not letting yourself half-arse it. Perhaps you've got some brain gunk clogging up your path to half-arse enlightenment. Let me grab a cotton bud and see if we can shift that for you . . .

GETTING EXCITED THAT YOU GET TO MAKE A DECISION AT ALL

Sometimes it feels like forks in the road are horrible disruptions or cruel jokes. They can make you feel sick, twist your insides into shrivelled knots, make you wish you weren't facing them.

I can bring myself back to reality by asking: what would this decision look like for me if I was making it a hundred years ago? In a different country? Having been born to different parents?

From abortions to birthday party venues, from divorces to which dentist to register with; most decisions have been hard-won by someone else long ago. Unfortunately, they're most likely dead but, if I'm being presumptuous, I would guess that they'd want you to use the autonomy they fought for and enjoy the delicious feeling of being free to make it. They didn't die/protest/consent to be mildly inconvenienced so that you would make the right decision. They were just pissed that you wouldn't get to make a decision at all. They knew you deserved to have that chance and that you were capable of it.

HANG-UPS ABOUT PREDESTINATION

The idea of the Butterfly Effect or films like *Sliding Doors* offer us great sweeping insights into how one small decision *can* send your life off in a completely different direction. It's an amazing concept to think about and makes for gripping cinema.

There has, however, been little evidence of this in my own life. Sure, there are a couple of honest-to-God moments of 'If I hadn't done _____ then I would never have met _____' or 'If I never _____ then the horrible event would never have occurred' – but I seriously doubt that every decision in life has a trajectory like that. We obviously can't know, but I would bet good money that a lot of decisions dictate the timing or specifics of a particular life event, but do not determine whether it happens *at all*.

What if I'd never accepted that place at university to study art, after years of planning to study business?

You may well have studied business for a year and realised what a colossal miserable mistake you'd made, and started that same art course, just a year later.

What if I'd never decided to go through my partner's phone when I had a hunch, I might have never known they were cheating and we'd be married by now?

Probably not, you're a smart cookie and I bet that eventually you'd have been able to smell the suspicious behaviour a mile off. There would have been other cracks emerging, and the relationship might have ended anyway.

If you're anything like me you might be able to trace your worry that there is a 'right path' for you, and that you might miss it, back to a religious sentiment. I grew up believing that God had a plan for my life and that it was my job to try to work out what that was and follow it. There were many options, but only one right choice: for my life partner, for my vocation, for almost everything. I spent a lot of time sitting there, waiting for God to tell me what to choose.

If he's ever spoken to you, that's great! Love that for you. However, it became apparent to me in my early twenties that I was being ghosted, and for various reasons, including that one, I decided that religion was not for me.

It took me a lot longer to realise that whenever I approached a fork in the road, I was often still looking for 'the plan' I had once believed so fervently in. As though it was just below the surface and all I had to do was excavate it. Any wrong turn could be a disastrous detour from 'my destiny' and every decision, however small, was crucial. Although I'd stopped believing in the plan *maker*, I had never faced the fact that there might not be a plan *at all*.

Even if you didn't grow up religious or don't currently have a faith, it's likely that you grew up in a country or a community who had some idea of 'predestination'. That someone was steering the ship. The idea of 'destiny' reigns over the secular and spiritual world in equal measure, in a way that's hard to spot. It can get under your skin and osmose into your psyche. You become like those fish who don't realise they're swimming in water.

While I no longer believed in a god, I hadn't taken time to unpick all of the underlying beliefs that came along with the concept of an omnipresent Sat Nav who had infinite wisdom and knew exactly what I should do with my life. Honestly, I miss it. It was kind of relaxing. Instead, I was lumped with little old chaotic MORTAL me in the driving seat and . . . I didn't trust her. It took a lot longer for me to process the fact that my life was mine to live, and there weren't as many wrong answers as I thought. In fact, I was *swimming* in right answers. Where a murky path through a dark forest once was, I now stood in an orchard of Cool Things To Do With My Life to pluck for myself, no supervision. While this is a freeing feeling, it's also understandable if you've lost your faith, in fate or God, that you might feel at sea about your own agency; about the thought that there really isn't a secret plan for your life filed away somewhere, unless *you* make one.

It's a good idea to lift the bonnet and check what kind of mouldy second-hand beliefs might have trickled in without you noticing.

Instead of picturing a sprawling star whose points represent the different directions your life could take at any given junction, I picture something more like a network of small decisions, some taking the scenic route, others the high-speed overpass, but often ending up at similar destinations.

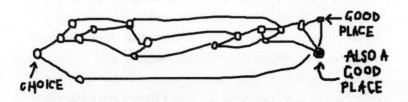

I don't think the universe is just flinging us about, I think it's more like a slow shuffle.

The decisions are permanent, yes, but you're not then hurtling towards a doomed future or paradise after every choice. You might make a great choice but fuck it up for yourself later: marrying the 'right' person but not maintaining the relationship, taking the 'best' job but getting arrogant and screwing up your opportunity. Luckily, the same is true of a 'bad' decision. You course correct as you go, you move lanes, you start indicating towards the right direction, even if you can't turn off the highway quite yet. If Jesus isn't taking the wheel, then the wheel is fair game, and you don't lose access to it after you make a big decision. You can keep driving.

YOU CAN LIVE THROUGH A BAD DECISION

Sometimes I think the fear we feel about the prospect of making the wrong decision isn't only connected to the external consequences of that decision, but also the emotional state we might be in afterwards. I fear regret in the same way I fear throwing up or getting the flu. It feels mysterious, horrifying, inevitable. Those aren't bad fears to have; in some ways I think this is a stealth showcasing of self-love. The thought of making my future self miserable as the result of a decision I'm about to make shows some sliver of self-preservation. In fact, procrastination about decision-making can neurologically be explained as a way for our brains to protect us from harm: if we're already in a low mood, the part of our brain that operates in the short term will think that avoiding dangerous negative emotions, or even the possibility of them, sounds like a great idea.

So, in some ways, if you're not worried about regret, I would be worried about *you*. If you're concerned about regret you clearly like yourself enough to want to preserve future-you's feelings.

But I also know that you can love someone and severely underestimate them.

Luckily there might be a way to have your cake and eat it too; by which I mean please both your present and your future selves.

Research has shown that self-determination plays a big role in being happy with an outcome. *The Journal of Personality and Social Psychology* published the research of Angus Campbell, which suggests that autonomy defined as, 'the feeling that your life – its activities and habits – are self-chosen and self-endorsed', was the highest predictor of happiness. According to Campbell, 'Having a strong sense of controlling one's life is a more dependable predictor of positive feelings of well-being than any of the objective conditions of life we have considered.'

So, potentially, if you just make a decision (good or bad) yourself, you're more likely to be content with the outcome than if you let circumstance or others make it for you.

Now go forth and make poor decisions, with my blessing!

DECISION FATIGUE

If, after all of that strategy and all of those pep-talks, you still want to throw your hands up and squeal *I don't know what to do!* . . . don't worry; you're in the right place.

Cognitive Load Theory lays out the strain we put on our minds in terms of information-processing systems. Just like with computers, too many tabs open in our brain means a general lag in processing time, especially when it comes to solving unfamiliar problems. We might normally be perfectly capable of weighing up a situation and making a decision, but if we're running too many of these problems through our 'working memory' at the same time (which is very clever but also has a limited capacity), we end up like the tiny wheel of doom on a frozen computer screen, spinning endlessly through time, towards despair and, eventually, death.

The more we can 'defrag' our brains and clear the cobwebs, the more room there is in our RAM to get the big things sorted. If we spend a whole lot of our day questioning every part of our lives; if we think *oh God, I'm cooking eggs again, am I an awful person?* as we make our breakfast; if we try to reinvent our personal style every time we get dressed; if we are constantly critiquing our personal waste every time we chew gum; if we spend our whole commute weighing up whether we're in the right job; if we return home only to try to recalibrate our living room into the perfect depiction of who we are as a person . . . there's not going to be much disk space left over for The Big Stuff, is there?

You're not bad at decisions, it's just that you're trying to make and re-make so many of them, all the time, without realising that you've used up all your decision-making superpowers. The supersoaker is empty.

The cognitive load is often referred to in workplace critiques of task-switching. Advocates for 'deep work' advise against too much multitasking in the workplace, and tell us that we'll get a lot more done if we stop lily-pad-hopping and focus on one thing at a time. I see no reason why we can't take this further and look at the rest of our lives the same way. We're so hyper-aware of all the ways we could be 'getting it wrong' in our everyday tasks and decisions – trying to go 'all in' and get every aspect of our choices 'right' and 'perfect' – that we become unable to even pick a priority, let alone get on with it.

To clear your hard drive, we'll need to sift through those folders of faff and fluff and make some room for a Big Processing Job. Perhaps the best way to do this is to tackle each area of your life as you might encounter it in everyday life, from morning to evening. So, first things first: while I love your choice of pyjamas, open your wardrobe – we're getting dressed . . .

Half-Arse Style

When I open my wardrobe doors, a lot of things come tumbling out onto the floor, literally and metaphorically. All my misguided purchases, failures of judgement, audacious experiments, best laid plaid-plans.

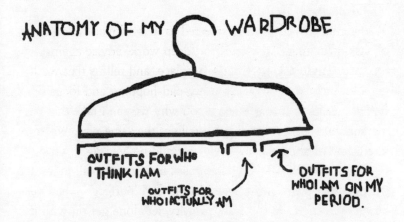

ANATOMY OF MY WARDROBE

OUTFITS FOR WHO I THINK I AM

OUTFITS FOR WHO I ACTUALLY AM

OUTFITS FOR WHO I AM ON MY PERIOD.

Held up by hangers as if to mock me, they are the ghosts of my dream selves I never actualised. Their seams wait to be wrapped around waistlines I had *no* business promising them. Their colours are far from harmonious, their styles everything from 'hungover children's TV presenter' to 'dishevelled Victorian tavern keeper'. I know that the closet inspectors aren't going to break down my door and mark my work with a big red pen (although if they did, I would be in deep shit). I know it isn't anyone else's business, that no one looks in there but me, but, regardless, I feel the weight of judgement every time I open those doors. I worry that the smattering of secret chaos behind them shows in the outfits I assemble from its rails, and that I leave the house looking like a skew-whiff scarecrow more often than I do a real human woman.

It's as though a spectre of Miranda Priestly (the beastly magazine editor from *The Devil Wears Prada*) is standing behind me, tutting.

She expected better of me.

THE CURSE OF PERSONAL STYLE

What *exactly* is it that Miranda wants to see? What *is* personal style? I've been getting some mixed messages. Here are a few of them.

A 'personal style' must be:

— Trendy BUT timeless
— Totally 'you' BUT assembled from items available off-the-rack in chain department stores
— Suit 'your shape' BUT also body positive
— Functional for your lifestyle BUT also elevated
— Neither 'too young' OR 'too old' for you
— Consistent BUT never repetitive

– Sustainable BUT affordable
– Showstopping BUT not *showy*

Oh feather of lead, oh loving-hate: these contradictions of Shakespearian proportions seem laughable when you lay them all out, and yet when they are dripped in gradually by the pipettes of media and culture, we don't realise that the task in hand has become absurd.

In essence, your personal style is a carefully curated wardrobe of trusty fashion accomplices that can drape you in 'wow factor', whatever the occasion. It should be honed, understated, specific. It must tell everyone, in no uncertain terms, who you are without you having to say a *word*.

Has anybody else spotted that wave of inevitable failure rolling towards us?

The remit for personal style feels like we're setting ourselves up for a faceplant . . . because we are. A deluge of closet clear-outs and style guides have been unsuccessful in helping us work out what we *actually* want. The average customer buys 60 per cent more garments *each year*. We then wear each item we buy around seven to ten times, before tossing it over our shoulder in favour of the next thing that is '*so* us'. In the UK, 49 per cent of all used textiles go straight in our general waste bins to either be incinerated or stuck in landfill. The fate of those clothes that are donated often isn't much better. Only 10–30 per cent of what is donated to charity shops actually gets sold. The rest of that either ends up in the bin, or is sold to textile merchants who resell them to places like the Kantamanto Market in Ghana, a destination that is often cited in documentaries and articles about the volume of waste we produce when we constantly 'spring clean' in the pursuit of this fabled perfect wardrobe. It's a place where the 'unwearables' of the Western donations market go to be sold for very little to those who deserve better. The act of popping a lot of unworn items in a bag for the charity shop can *feel* noble, like we're doing the world a favour, but in actuality, so poor is the quality of what we 'donate', 40 per cent of what ends up in these kinds of markets goes into landfill. Locally, the clothes are referred to as '*broni we wu*' or 'the white person has died' – because, they reason, what kind of living person would throw out so much stuff? The only excuse must be kicking the bucket.

And yet here we are, alive. Alive and clicking. Ready to lap up advice from whatever half-baked article or influencer that can promise us that final synergy, that end point at which shopping will be 'done'. That the task of explaining ourselves on our bodies *will* be completed. I am starting to suspect the myth of the elusive wardrobe formula is as hopeless as the search for Atlantis, yet we'll keep diving until the oxygen runs out.

You'll have to lend me a hand so I can swing myself down off my high horse, though, because I, too, lap up every single article. I've watched every video. I believe in the lost city, and, when I find it, I believe I'll have the perfect outfit in which to strut through its soggy streets.

Can all of this be put down to personal delusion? Or are there larger powers at hand? Sure, most cultures throughout history have emphasised the importance of looks, so what makes this era different? Perhaps it's not, but I do think there is something uniquely sinister about the way we're currently pushed to market ourselves like a product at a faster pace than ever before.

The average person is almost forced to mentally do an advertising exercise every time they assemble a LinkedIn, Hinge or Instagram profile. From online dating to Facebook-founded community spaces, personality hires and digital side-hustles, the appeals of personal branding can bleed into our professional and personal life.

Which three words do I want people to associate with me?

What colours best communicate that 'vibe'?

Which of the thousands of pictures that exist of me will give the impression that I am *that* person?

Even if you're not a public figure, there is a pressure to hone a 'personal brand', as though you were in a line-up to join the Spice Girls. Amongst our friends we're no longer simply predictable, or our actions 'so us'; we're 'on brand'. As technology and poor workplace etiquette ensure that our personal and professional lives bleed into each other, as a cost-of-living crisis forces us to create side hustles in our 'spare' time to supplement our income, it's no wonder our minds begin to think like marketeers. Our brains were designed to exist in a group of one hundred or so people, so it's little wonder how overwhelmed we are to be reminded every day of how large our animal groups have become, and how unremarkable we are within that vast soup of human activity. Think of the numbers next to the memes we interact with online ('*988.5k people have liked this post*'); the statistics shared in the news every day ('*100,000 people's pensions are forecasted to be worth less due to . . .*'); and even the streaming services show how many times our intimately loved favourite songwriter's ballad has played in the ears of other people (*48 million streams*). The more we are aware of how small we are, how many multiples there must be of us out there, the stronger is our drive to either 'stand out' and be 'memorable', or blend in for safety, lest the group turn on us.

For me, the promise of personal style is not only to help me 'stand out'; it's also the promise of a kind of sophistication that I innately *don't* possess. I often feel crumpled, grubby, a little *mossy*, even. I want a wardrobe that will shield me from all the things I fear I am: impermanent, rickety, all over the place, perpetually on the verge of rotting. I've come to realise that over the years in which I was searching for my style, when my mouth said 'sophistication' my brain meant:

refined, intelligent, affluent.

But did I really *want* to be seen as any of these things? Do I even *agree* with them as concepts? Do they align with who I am fighting tooth and nail to become?

Let's take them one by one, and see why, really, I disagree with myself.

INTELLIGENT: I believe that intelligence doesn't *really* have any visual signals. I know the archetypes, but surely they should stay in poorly shot eighties movies, where they belong? Tweed blazers, well cut two-pieces, tailored skirts, polished shoes. Things that signify an era of well-behaved class politics that we're trying to usher out. At best they're a bit silly, at worst they're pretty classist. Most importantly, they're just wrong. If I was to wear something that successfully made someone who had never spoken to me think I was smart, that person would be using flawed logic and potentially be a bit of a spanner. They'd be someone I wouldn't want to get to know. So why am I pre-emptively buying clothes, ready for their once-over?

AFFLUENT: When it comes to 'looking affluent', I come up empty-handed too. I actively **don't like** the idea that some people have astronomically more money than other people, and I think it's weird when people try to dress as if they are rich (whether or not they have the wallet to match).

REFINED: a word, have you noticed, that is flattering when it's used about someone's style, but negative in any other context. Malt syrup, fructose, corn sweetener, dextrose – they're all types of refined sugar we're told to consume only in small doses, to avoid in breakfast cereal, to beware of using regularly. It's a type of sweetness that has *come from* a natural source, but has been processed so rigorously that only a few components of its original flair remain. If 'refined' means having all my delicious bits boiled out, you can keep it.

The popularity of style signifiers like this have been magnified in recent years with the rise of trends like 'Clean Girl', 'Dark Academia', 'Old Money' and many more. They each come with dubious connotations around hygiene and aspirations for an old, musty kind of structural power.

Your descriptive words might be different. What do you think about what you associate with your perfect 'personal style' honed wardrobe? Classic? Edgy? Minimalist? Chic? Alternative? Elegant? It's worth writing them down and seeing what you really mean when you say them. Asking yourself if you *really want* to be those things, or be seen that way, and why. Are their aesthetics genuinely pleasing to you, or are they just a way of avoiding being perceived as something you fear being, such as scatty, grubby, out of place? Of course, there's nothing wrong with a spotless cashmere sweater or a sharply ironed tennis skirt, as long as the people donning them are wearing them to spark joy in themselves rather than intimidate others.

The problem with 'branding' is that, just like 'refined', it has negative connotations in any other context. It either refers to the marker of a product that can be mass produced and sold off to anyone who wants it. Not ideal. OR it refers to the literal branding of livestock; beings whose purpose it is to serve, and who must be branded so as to mark out who they belong to.

I'm going to be honest; it's not looking appealing.

THE CON OF THE CAPSULE WARDROBE

A 'capsule wardrobe' is a concept coined in the 1970s by Susie Fox, the owner of the London boutique Wardrobe, and is widely accepted as referring to a limited collection of clothes that can be endlessly interchanged with each other to make up an impressive number of outfits. The emphasis is often on quality, neutrality and the elusive 'essence' of the person curating it. It's also been held up in recent years as the main tool for building a more sustainable wardrobe, something we're becoming increasingly anxious about (because of, you know, the lava).

To assemble one, you must first know your 'personal style'. Each item is meticulously selected in accordance with that ineffable essence, no room for dead weight. Each item must earn its keep. There's the 333 method (three tops, three bottoms, three pairs of shoes which can be combined into twenty-seven outfits), the 10 x 10 challenge (wearing ten items in various combinations for ten days at a time), the Rule of 5 (five of every type of item, no more), the 54321 system (five tops, four bottoms, three accessories, two shoes, one swimsuit) – but whichever one you choose, the emphasis is on LESS.

Sounds great right? Less money spent, less time needed and, presumably, much better for the planet too.

The problem comes when you try to *find* those few sacred perfect items. No one gets to perfection without a few prototypes and failed auditions. Although the capsule wardrobe was brought into being in the 1970s, its real heyday has been the past five years. On TikTok #capsulewardrobe has 700 million views and you can't open Instagram without being served videos of various influencers shimmying across the screen in their various combinations of beige peg leg trousers and navy knitwear.

Interestingly, during that same time period, Britons have been chucking out an average of seventy-two items of clothing a year per person and spending around 57.8 billion per year on new clothes. If pared-down personal style is the cure to our overconsumption ills, I'm afraid we're very much still clogged with phlegm.

What I've found, from my own experiments in attempting to build a 'capsule' collection, is that when you don't have access to an expensive stylist or a personal tailor, more trial and error is required than these style experts let on. Emphasis on the error. Much like the trend of minimalism creating as much landfill as collective 'zen', my hunch is that the average capsule wardrobe we see online has all the aesthetics of scarcity, without the results. Below the cool surface of a spacious clothes rail is the girthy underbelly of an iceberg. The twenty discarded pairs of jeans we must purchase before we land on 'the one'. The five 'little black dresses' that turned out to be too little, too black, too dressy.

The ten tan tank tops that were all ordered to our doorstep only to be posted back the next day (did you know that 80 per cent of clothing returns are never resold by brands? It's cheaper to bin them than use employee time to check they're not damaged).

It's worth sniffing our failed attempts and starting to question if perhaps there's something strange about the style advice we've been swimming in . . . does something smell fishy to you?

Come to think of it, the only other times I've heard the term 'capsule' in normal conversation is when I was burying a lunchbox as a 'time capsule' school project, or someone in a film was sealing something precious away in a controlled environment (Alien plasma? A severed human hand? A sealed pod to rocket into outer space?). It creates a static, sterile environment that functions to preserve things. Not a bad use of technology for a science experiment or a plot device, but it doesn't sound like the breeding ground for a 'drop dead' outfit, unless you're thinking literally not figuratively.

The waste (both of your time, and of global resources) comes when you follow the advice of the elusive capsule wardrobe experts. For a capsule wardrobe to be successful, each item within it must interchangeably match with every other item of clothing, and so their compatibility needs to be carefully planned out. This, in theory, will bring you a large number of combinations, in the hundreds, so you always look 'new' whilst still wearing the same small number of items.

Again, I have reservations about how effective this can be in preserving both our sanity and the planet. Surely it stands to reason that if you view your wardrobe as if it were a carefully cast film, where absolutely everyone needs to have 'chemistry', where the right people need to look related, where no one can age above their character during the filming window . . . you're going to run into problems.

When you remove a card, the whole tower topples.

If there's a role in your wardrobe for a green jacket, great. When your favourite one wears out, you can find another. If the role specifically calls for '*a tapered moss-green jacket with flared sleeves and a composition of 89 per cent linen and 11 per cent spandex*', what happens when you can't find that item again?

The capsule wardrobe is exactly the kind of idea that is well intentioned, but can result in a kind of 'yoyo' relationship with our wardrobe that forces us into a constant cycle of clearing out and restocking that results in the mountains of garment waste piling up in landfill and waste-ridden markets across the world.

We need to stop trying to freeze our 'dream team' of garments in time and start assembling a wardrobe that's more like a daytime soap opera – bring in the archetypes, get ready for a couple of decades of action, be ready to swap out The Dad without caring two hoots if the actors vaguely resemble each other.

It's not only the composition of a capsule wardrobe that I don't think we should be arsed with. I wonder if size matters as much as they imply? What is the benefit of keeping our wardrobes small, besides the physical limits of our storage?

Sure, if I had a time machine and I could rewind back to before the industrial revolution, I would definitely try to persuade the powers that be to avoid trying to build a world in which there are a thousand times more pieces of clothing on earth than people. But I don't have a time machine, the clothes have been made, and I am more than willing to keep second-hand items in my wardrobe if it means not sending them to landfill. Having a smaller collection might have a practical benefit for you; you might like to travel frequently, or have limited storage, or a full rack of clothes makes you anxious. Beyond that, as the clothes already exist, I do not see what the planet has to gain from us having such a strictly controlled collection of clothes.

In fact, the more clothes that are kept in circulation, above ground, however rarely we might wear them, the better. What matters is the rate at which we accumulate *new* items, and in what manner those textiles have been made.

And what kind of pressure, I wonder, might make us feel as though we urgently need an incredibly specific list of clothing items that we couldn't possibly find, or wait to arrive, in the second-hand market?

Oh, I don't know, something like the pressure to build, in one burst of frantic activity, a capsule wardrobe.

CLOTHES ARE NOT TIMELESS, THEY ARE DYING SLOWLY LIKE THE REST OF US

The messaging becomes even more confusing when we layer it over the pressure to follow trends, to watch out for those parts of our wardrobe that are 'out' and be constantly open to introducing items that are 'in'.

The solution we're handed is 'timeless' fashion.

Except . . . it rarely is. Just like with the rest of fashion, 'staple' pieces fall in and out of favour too. The cut of a trench coat, the width of a jean leg, the length of a skirt. These, as much as the bright green feather skirt or the loud polka dot dress, are all susceptible to trend cycles and changing preferences.

Clothes are, in some ways, living objects in that they change, they stretch, they bobble, they wear, they decay. Anyone who has known the chasm left in the soul by the discovery that a well-loved jumper is now unravelling, appreciates that. Even the most sturdy of suspects is here for a good time, not a long time. The bodies they are made for fluctuate too. We shift, we age, we shrink, we grow – humans are relentless, wiggling things. We don't even have the same skin each decade, for goodness' sake. All the cells in our body regenerate on a cycle of about seven years: *we're literally not the same person.*

Knowing what we do about the transience of textiles and the bodies they're meant to cover, it makes you wonder why we ever set out on this quest. Indeed, if 'timeless' fashion were possible, there would be no intrigue in vintage pieces, no charm to old films, no 'moment' the piece was trying to capture. We must remember that, however diluted, every item of clothing has been designed by someone. Fashion, for all its faults and high jinks, is art. And art is a record of the maker's taste, their vantage point on the world and the time they made it in. To ask a designer to create something 'timeless' is like asking a chef to make something without flavour, or an architect to design a building that will never age.

Better to reconcile ourselves with what an item is, and to the possibility that whoever sees us in it *might* be able to guess when we bought it, or at least when it was made. Unless you're mingling daily with fashion historians or style influencers, they probably won't give a monkey's.

Let's look at some half-arse attitudes to clothes that might clear some space in your brain, if not your rails. Pick one, or combine a few, whatever helps you halve your style stress and gets you back out there . . .

IT'S NOT A WARDROBE, IT'S A DRESS-UP BOX

Another thing I find daunting about the concept of personal style is the idea that I don't actually *know* myself. What if I'm not failing at item selection, or refining my taste, or if it's not simply because I haven't looked hard enough for the perfect item? What if I don't really know who I am? What if, underneath all the clothes, there is *no one to know?*

The question of whether or not we are knowable is one I'll leave to the philosophers, but from my experience, my 'self' has always been a slippery thing. It won't be nailed to the floor, and trying to pin it down only results in tears and torn skin. I've accepted that I change all the time and thus being my own stylist is a thankless task.

In actual fact, my most positive memories with clothes growing up come from those heightened moments of playing pretend. The dress-up box at a friend's house, that obnoxious skirt loaned from the theatre department for a production of a school play (probably sewn by someone else's long-suffering mum), the Halloween costume held together by safety pins and parental prayers.

In those moments no one was wondering if what I was wearing was practical or if it 'worked' for me. The remit was clear: I was wearing what I was wearing so I could better resemble a queen/cow/muddy peasant/toothpaste tube (yes, I went to a Halloween party as a toothpaste tube, it was the only way my classmates' pagan party would wash with my religious parents). I wasn't tricking anyone. The outfit didn't promise authenticity, it promised play. *And play I did.*

Once I started to think of myself as more of a costume mistress, things started falling into place.

The memories that stick out to you from your childhood might not be the same. The moments where you might have felt most harmonious with your clothes might have been when you were walking towards a stadium wrapped in a striped scarf, feeling the fizzing power of wearing colours that meant you belonged. It might have been while wearing something handmade just for you, and feeling the rush of knowing that there was only one item like that in the world. Maybe it was donning something that made it possible for you to dance, or swim, or climb. Whatever it was, it's worth giving that memory a good shake and seeing what lessons fall out. It might shift your hunch on how to *really* reach that feeling of harmony that the pursuit of personal style promises, but rarely delivers.

Particularly within recent online culture, our demands for sincerity have reached undeliverable heights: we want our musicians to sing about their own lives so we can dissect their relationships; we want to know our favourite comedians' politics; we want to know what's in our favourite actor's handbag. We inspect celebrities' paparazzi pictures hoping that the clothes they (supposedly) choose for themselves will help us learn more about who they really are, 'off-stage'. There is so much that matters about the way we all communicate, I just don't think that personal style is one of the most important ones. It's not worth being arsed about. It's almost as though we've started believing that wearing something that doesn't reflect our personality equates to being disingenuous – that our clothes can't represent *anything but* our own essence.

I refuse to accept that the age of the dress-up box is over. The most truthful thing about me is that I like to mess about. I like to play.

My suggestion is, instead of trying to guess which aspects of our personality or temperament are here to stay, we should think about what *else* could inspire some consistency in our wardrobes. Whilst favourite colours and lovers and postcodes have shifted, two passions have remained constant so far in my life: Helena Bonham Carter and *The Sound of Music*.

I realised that some of the longest-serving items amongst my monster pile of clothes weren't the ones that fit me the best, or were in my 'colour palette' – but the ones that made me feel like I might be minutes from speeding through the Austrian mountains on a bike pursued by seven singing children, or was about to spend my evening pulling pints in a steampunk pub surrounded by revolutionaries. Perhaps you have your own equivalent? Maybe you want to always look like you've just fallen out of a Frida Kahlo painting, or a Beyoncé video, or been rolled out of William Morris' curtains.

It's not by accident that the art we love conjures clear aesthetics in our minds – they've been designed that way. The work has been done for us. Painters have palettes, films have costume designers, music artists have creative teams. Streamline your stress by making a list of visual worlds you've always felt drawn to, despite the trends coming and going, and choose your clothes accordingly. I promise harmony will follow, no maths equation required.

STORIES OVER STYLE

I realise that for several pages I've been lambasting personal style, but I do think we've got a fighting chance of rectifying it as a concept, as long as we expand its definition and half-arse the hell out of it.

For example, while many might argue there should be an emphasis on wearing pieces that 'match', I actually believe one of the key markers of a good outfit is an unexpected item that isn't in harmony with the rest. Where else are we going to get that 'pop' that stylists go on about? My favourite items on other people aren't the ones that prompt the response, 'Thanks, I got it in the sale for a FIVER!', but the ones that prompt a personal story.

Thanks, I got it from this weird outdoor Welsh market on the same weekend my girlfriend proposed to me.

Aw, I've actually had this since I was a teenager, so weird I know – have I ever told you what a total knob I was at fifteen?!

Aw thank you, it has HUGE pockets, can I show you what's in my HUGE pockets, so many things [proceeds to monologue a commentary of the fifty-nine things you pull from the inner guts of your coat, like handkerchiefs from a magician's hat].

The definition we discussed at the beginning of the chapter, of personal style as something to tell everyone 'who you are without you having to say a word' is actually kind of sad on reflection. Because I like saying words. I like gaggle gatherings and shouty nights out and whispered conspiracies and long phone calls and snappy catch-ups and funny exchanges with strangers on the train. I like the idea that *I actually have to* talk to someone before I know them. That I can't get it all in a glance from the pleat of a peplum skirt or the flush of a fluorescent fleece. That I won't know whether you're a particular sort of person from the type of green you wear, or whether your statement piece is a chunky necklace or a cross-body bag.

I'm not saying the idea of 'personal style' is a conspiracy to stop us all from actually talking to each other, but I'm not NOT saying that either.

And, of course, without visual shorthands, things become more limited. We can't know *everyone* at a glance. Maybe that's okay. Who has a personality that can be perfectly distilled into an ensemble of striped tops and staple socks? And what would that person *be* like? Would you want them at your hen do?

'Kelly was a proper laugh, but that Rachel woman has the personality of a *trench coat*!'

I think it's okay to remain a mystery to onlookers. To accept that our clothes don't have to reflect who we are, all of the time. That perhaps we're raw sugar, too complicated to be boiled down and refined into colour palettes and silhouettes and textures. What if an item of clothing could become part of your personal style purely on the merit basis of it being in some way personal to *you*?

I have a red top that I am aware doesn't suit me at all – but whenever I look down, I feel powerful. I have a jumpsuit that has mysteriously fit me at every size, from an 18 to a 12; I know it's not alive but I feel so UNjudged by it, it honestly feels radical. Every time I pull it over my hips it winks at me as if to say 'You're back! Lucky me!' I have a coat in my wardrobe that is there purely for its huge pockets. That,

alone, is what makes me reach for it. There's this pair of
wide-leg cotton trousers I was wearing the day I was in an
almost fatal car crash. Flimsy as they are, they stood between
broken glass and skin as I climbed out of an upside-down
car; they kept me cool as I sat on the hot tarmac in the
middle of a motorway, waiting for an ambulance that would
tell me, miraculously, that I was fine.

You've heard the argument that every body is a beach body:
by dint of being a body and being on the beach. Well, what
if everything you wear *is* your personal style, by dint of it
being on your person?

Your personal style might be more about the sensory feel
of the clothes you wear than the look of them, and that's
what makes them personal. It might be what they allow you
to do, the range of movement they give you. Your personal
style might simply be: busy. Too busy to pick a good outfit.
Not choosing is a choice in itself, so, ta-dah – that *is still*
personal style!

In the same vein, I think a piece of clothing can become
your 'personal style' if it was acquired in a way that aligns
with what you believe. It might be your style because it's
second hand, and you personally believe in that. It might be
that you bought it from a small independent brand, or
directly from the maker themselves. I like to think that most
people, given the choice, are kind. It is a marvel that we've
been convinced that, irrespective of the needless waste and
human exploitation involved in the making of most
garments, we can walk into a high street fast-fashion shop
and gasp at a dress that is 'so us'. As I learned more about

the way the clothes that hung in the shops I frequented made it there, I started to wonder: if an item was made in a way that makes me so instinctually sad, how 'me' can it really be?

Instead of berating ourselves for not having a perfectly ethical, sustainable or visually succinct wardrobe, what would it be like to set fewer parameters for perfection; perhaps it's enough to simply search for things that *feel* personal. The more I learned about the way clothes are produced, the less attached to the brands I felt, the less buzz I got from being on their websites. I no longer have that manufactured feeling of comfort or 'home' walking through the doors of H&M. I didn't need to go cold turkey or make rules for myself, it was a slow breakup; the spark faded, we wanted different things. I gradually started to feel in my bones that it wasn't right. It was no longer 'me'.

Just like people, the items in your wardrobe might not tick every box. They might have rickety parts and off days and sauce down their chin. Despite that, something about the way they laugh, or look at the world, or the fact that you went through *the hard thing* together, means that you're in it for life. If we widen the remit of what is 'allowed' in our wardrobe, we make it more sustainable without even trying, and, even better, it can free up brain space we can use for whatever we want.

STOP SEARCHING, START SEWING

Learning a whole new skill might seem like an odd suggestion when it comes to streamlining your relationship to clothes, but I have found learning some simple sewing and knitting techniques to be a way of quieting the conundrums that shop-bought fashion throws at me. I can no longer be arsed to traipse between shops, trying to find the jacket that sits 'just right' – I'm simply learning (once, to be used for my whole life) the technique of altering the jacket so it fits the way I wish they had designed it to fit. Instead of seeking out and spending money on five occasion-dresses that all have one or two things I like about them, I have frankensteined my preferences into a single fit-all-occasion dress that has the perfect amount of give, colour, swish and, most importantly, pockets.

It's also a great way to form that 'friendship' with my clothes that I described. My warmest jumper becomes the one I knitted, sitting next to my mum, on a long train journey to Scotland. My favourite linen shirt is the one I rush-sewed before spending a special New Year's Eve with my old school friends. My favourite summer dress, which I unpicked and re-sewed three times, becomes an emblem of triumph against my own negative self-talk because, lumpy and uneven as it is, it exists. As I accept its flaws, I am more forgiving of my own.

Knitting is also the perfect distraction for your hands, to stop you from scrolling shopping sites – in this AK season of my life (known as After [I discovered] Knitting) I look back at those times of endless browsing in BK (Before Knitting) and think: *did I want new clothes or was I just fidgeting?!* Who knew that all that wriggling could create clothes I really loved? That I would never dream of returning or selling on? The only way my hand-knitted mustard and pink-striped wool jumper is going to landfill is if they bury it with my decaying body. All hail the Productive Fidget.

A nice contradiction to my point about capsule wardrobes being a delicate house of cards is that, if you learn to sew and you keep your patterns around, there's a very real chance that you CAN return to that much fetishised idea of a capsule wardrobe – since when one of your actors drops out, you can fix them up and send them back out there or literally clone a new cast member from an almost identical fabric.

THE ART OF THE MUSHROOM WARDROBE

Have you ever read about mushrooms? How, from the soil up, they all look like separate, sassy little guys in their smart little hats, but underneath they're all connected, holding hands, whispering? Merlin Sheldrake's work on mushrooms has changed the way we all see fungi for ever, and his book *Entangled Life* is particularly interesting. What we might see on the surface of the soil are single mushrooms, but below ground they're in fact part of a mycelial network so intricate and intertwined that it's hard to venture that there is such a thing as an 'individual mushroom'.

That's my vision for the future of local wardrobes. That, to the untrained eye, we all surface from our homes as individual, goodlooking, stylish mushrooms – but secretly, below the soil, there are hundreds of networks connecting our wardrobes, sending signals and swapping gladrags.

You see, the danger of a very specific personal style is that it detracts from our ability to do what Teen Leena loved best: SWAPSIES. Back when I lived in the pockets of my friends and we were forever lounging on each other's beds, poking through each other's stuff, I (accidentally) had a much more sustainable and less stressful approach to style. Four of us could get ready for a party from one person's wardrobe, no questions asked. Every time I went to stay with my best friend in another city, we'd usually leave with a different set of clothes to the ones we came in, having bartered for temporary loan of the perfect faux leather jacket, or a beaded tank top. Having no sisters of my own, the occasions I was summoned to rifle through bin bags filled by a friend's older sister's clear out were, to me, like clothes Christmas. Planet Noughties Tweenage Girl was a universe with limited financial resources, narrow hanging space and a shared ache to look as cool as humanly possible. The choice was clear: band together or face the bitter apathy of the masses. Possessiveness was not an option, we *had* to become a network. This continued into my twenties, living in a ramshackle big house with six other girls during university, where assembling the resources for a dress-up party or a night out required no more effort than swinging open your bedroom door and shouting your demands into the stairwell.

I've found, though, that as we get older the tone of wardrobe etiquette starts to change: we don't feel like we should 'bother' people, it feels 'cheap' to ask to borrow items that we perhaps should be purchasing ourselves, 'swapsies' starts to feel childish.

Well, I'm here to declare swapsies timeless!

Whether you've experienced something similar to my teenage years or you haven't and you feel you've been cheated, I'm here to tell you that there is still time. Make your mushroom wardrobe by creating little invisible strings between your wardrobe and those of the people around you. If you don't have close friends that are your dress size or have your personal style, throw that net wider. I've thrown swap parties at my house and encouraged plus ones, joined Facebook groups full of friendly strangers, logged on to buy-nothing forums, done appeals on my social media for items I need to borrow or that need a new home. There are lots of apps and local initiatives to get involved with that will help you grow links beneath the soil of your style . . . just watch what blooms when you make fashion fungal!

A HALF-ARSE CHECKLIST FOR YOUR PERSONAL STYLE

It strikes me that a lot of authors say, when asked for advice on creating a book, that their book isn't made and *then* edited, but that the book is made *in* the edit. My experience of building a wardrobe I love has been similar. Getting dressed is fingerpainting, it's just a rough draft of who you are, what you're going through. The choices you make, the selection process you use: they *are* you; if you made the choice, it's your style! That's it!

If you'd like a framework to plug into, a half-arse way to decide whether a piece of clothing is your personal style, have a look through the list below. If it checks HALF the boxes, you should take it home.

❑ it was made in a way I agree with
❑ if I hung it on my wall like a piece of art, I wouldn't get sick of looking at it
❑ it reminds me of something I've loved for a long time (film, painting etc.)
❑ it feels good to wear, according to my own definition of 'good'
❑ it will spark playful conversations with people
❑ I would wear it even if I wasn't going to see another human all day

And, before I send you back out into a world of clothes hauls and cursed fashion trends, here are some mantras for your back pocket. Repeat after me:

We are not our wardrobes.

You will never look exactly like yourself.

A capsule wardrobe is a fool's errand.

You don't have a moral obligation to wear clothes that match.

'Building' a wardrobe is not a completable task.

You already have a personal style.

The French are often held up by the rest of the world as the epitome of personal style, citing their lack of reverence for trends, and 'effortless' outfits. Those of us who aren't French are (ironically) encouraged to pore over manuals of how to achieve the same kind of weightless flair. Surely if we study it, we can achieve it? There must be some kind of crackable code?

Yet when you actually ask a stylish French person, for example the fashion photographer Garance Doré, they say things like 'elegance is refusal'.

So, I invite you to join me in trying something new: actually listening to the people who are supposedly getting it 'right'. If they say refuse, refuse. Refuse to over-study style, refuse to part with your money, to have someone else tell you what's stylish and what's not, refuse to care as much as they want you to.

The secret to effortless style might be, after all that, simply putting in less effort.

Which is just as well, because we're about to be late for work . . .

Half-Arse Career

—

Call it what you want: a job, a profession, a trade, a 'calling'. . . the most accurate of all the employment terms has to be 'occupation'.

Like it or desperately want to lump it, it is what *occupies* you.

For most people, it occupies a large chunk of their time as a 'grown up'. Eighty thousand hours, on average, to be precise. For others it also lays claim to their thoughts, worries and dreams. It's what preoccupies them in the quiet moments between mouthfuls. It's what grows through the cracks of the rest of their day, even when they're not 'on the clock'. Like romantic relationships, it's something we're supposed to yearn for from a young age.

What do you want to be when you grow up?, we coo at the poor tiny bastards who are simply trying to enjoy their Curly Wurlys in peace.

It's also work, and how successful we are at being recruited for it, that dictates our ability to occupy a house, a town or sometimes even a country. It can determine who we meet, who we marry, how many children we can afford to have. What we fill our days with, and how much it pays, is the key that unlocks our access to basic needs like shelter, food and water. It's often what dictates how healthy we are, how our brains develop and, ultimately, how happy half of our waking hours are.

So . . . not a thing to half-arse, right?

Except throwing our whole arse into work has proved to have some pretty dire consequences.

Mind, the leading mental health charity in the UK, found that work was the leading cause of stress in people's lives, surpassing debt, financial problems and health. 25 per cent of people surveyed had considered resigning due to mental pressure at work, 57 per cent said they drink after the workday to cope, and 14 per cent said they drink *during* it. Behind alcohol as a coping method was smoking (27 per cent), antidepressants (15 per cent) and prescribed sleeping tablets (10 per cent). 18 per cent said they had developed anxiety issues due to their workplace environment, and 7 per cent of workers said it had caused suicidal thoughts (this figure goes up to 10 per cent amongst 18–24-year-olds).

According to the Chartered Institute of Personnel and Development (CIPD), who looked at absence due to sickness across 6.5 million employees and 918 organisations, 76 per cent of workers had to take time off in 2023 due to workplace stress. So widespread is its rise that in 2019 burn-out was included as a specifically occupational phenomenon in the eleventh revision of the International Classification of Diseases.

Of course, there are worse conditions in some parts of the world, and much better in others. There have also been worse times to be a waged worker in history . . . but I've recently come to understand that it doesn't need to be this way, nor has it always. For example, researchers suggest that the average English peasant in the fourteenth century only put in around 150 days of work per year, usually with room for a little *nap* during the day. A *nap*. That's a three-day work week! WITH NAPS! Sure, life was awful in a myriad of other ways (they still ended up revolting, after all), but still . . .

As living standards have fallen for both working and middle-class households across the planet, stock market values have continued to hit all-time highs. The world welcomed 149 new billionaires in 2023! The problem isn't that we are not working hard enough. Rather, we're *overworking* while having the fruits of our productivity siphoned off before we can cover all of our basic bases. We've started to accept that we all have to bust our arses on behalf of those at the top who can't be arsed. And that's where a little half-arse fairy dust comes in. Realistically, a more manageable life for most can't be found behind the magic door marked 'work your arse off and rise to the top'. It's behind the one that says 'win the right to be fairly compensated for what you do and watch your work shifts halve'.

But, I hear you ask, *even if we achieved that, what would we do with all that extra time?* Isn't having a career a central part of who we are? Would we be fulfilled if we didn't throw everything we had in to it?

There's also a hole in this logic when we remember (lest we are unable to forget) that 'keeping occupied' isn't something most of us struggle with. We have plenty that would fill our time, even if we didn't have to turn up to work. Millions of people are *more* than occupied with the rearing of children, the nursing of the elderly, giving care to those who need care that otherwise wouldn't come. They might be caring for their own body, which demands round-the-clock admin, and very little energy to do it with. They might be unpicking an addiction or habit or a haunting that almost leads to their demise on a daily basis. These vital things that fill our time might not be something we're financially compensated for, but fill our time all the same.

The undercurrent of disdain wafted towards anyone who is 'otherwise occupied', and who also struggles to fit in the 'right' kind of labour alongside the other ways they are working, as if they simply 'can't be arsed', is at best, *very silly*. I would wager that there are very few people who are 'half-arsing', 'part-timing' or 'unemployed' that aren't otherwise engaged in projects of equal importance. It would be more accurate to assert that someone is simply 'unwaged' rather than unemployed, as so much of life outside of the workplace demands the employment of a huge amount of effort.

It's for this reason that I whole-heartedly endorse the intentional half-arsing of employment for anyone who is also throwing themselves into something else that is incredibly necessary. After all, we live in a world where the more necessary a task is, the less likely it is to be lucrative.

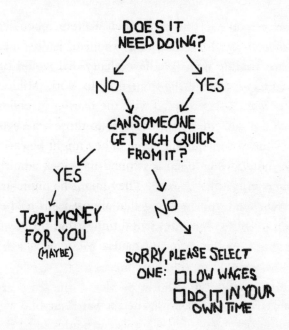

There are so many things that need doing outside of the world of parenting, care and recovery that are also *unwaged*. But it's hard to believe that the Venn diagram of 'what makes money' and 'what actually needs doing' contains very many jobs at all. Just look at the thousands of voluntary projects and organisations that run on gumption and prayers; communities around the world sticky-taped together by free labour, given readily in the pursuit of GOOD THINGS for people they might not know, or never meet.

In the UK we have 11,000 charity shops (that's about ten per town), all of which would not be open without an army of 'retired' people who simply refuse, if at all avoidable, to sit on their arses. We have over 2,500 food banks, 50,000 library volunteers, 30,000 Scout and Guide groups, 4,600 weekly Alcoholics Anonymous meetings, 10,000 amateur theatre shows are staged every year . . . all upheld by the unpaid labour of people who refuse to see the world arsed up, even if it means lending their time in exchange for company and diluted orange squash rather than cold hard cash.

It's for this reason that I am fascinated by the 'I do not dream of labour' meme that went viral in 2019 as a retort to the question 'what is your dream job?', as well as the conversations that it sparked. It became a commentary about how capitalism shapes our dreams and desires (which I agree is a problem) but morphed into unhelpfully vague slogans about preferring to be inactive or to opt out of society, exacerbated by the think pieces on the Great Resignation – a period of a few pandemic-riddled years in which a vast amount of workers quit their jobs . . . including me.

In a world where work isn't necessarily going to fulfil you, supply your life with meaning, provide your community with the improvements it needs, or furnish your brain with creative freedom, can I interest you in something cooler? Here is my half-arse approach to career balance . . .

THE PERFECT WORKPLACE DOES NOT EXIST (BUT YOU HAVE TO CHOOSE ONE ANYWAY)

The catchphrase:

'Do what you love and you'll never work a day in your life'*

sounds wonderful, but I bet you've never squinted to read the small print:

*'Apply to do what you love and end up spending most of your day doing stuff you don't love but is tangentially connected to the thing that you once loved, and also feel disheartened at the thought that you now know the inner workings of the industry that upholds the thing you once loved and can see all the ways the thing is being ruined by soggy systems and rotten rails.'

Less catchy, but had *that* been the inspirational quote plastered on the wall of the career adviser's office at my school it would have saved me a lot of time when choosing a career.

To me, there are three categories of workplace satisfaction:

Like what you do
Like what you're doing it for
Like the way you're doing it

I'd love to tell you to ONLY take a job that offers you all three, but, honestly, you'll be lucky if you get one. That's the reality for most people on earth. However, I think deciding which one is most important to you, and mitigating the damage of the other two factors, is your best bet. Plenty of people live glittering, whole, happy lives with just one of these ticked off.

Half-arse job satisfaction is most definitely on the cards for you! Let's take a look at each one, and weigh up the pros and cons of each.

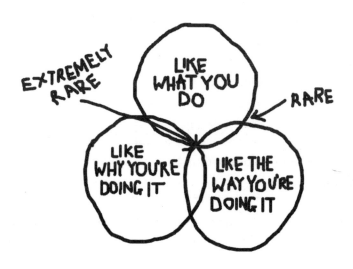

LIKE WHAT YOU DO

This is the initial route you're ushered down if you've ever been to a careers workshop at school. An activity that comes naturally to you, that you happen to be quite good at and happens to also be an occupation that someone will pay you for. Just as Hercule Poirot is passionate about solving murders and Popeye was born to be a sailor, you might be amongst those lucky few whose vocation floats down into their lap like an autumn leaf. The pros of liking what you do should need little explaining but . . .

THE PROS OF LIKING WHAT YOU DO

You get to do the thing you like doing! You get energy from the way it excites you, and it endlessly fascinates you, as do new ways to master and refine it. You might have colleagues that are ready-baked compatible friends, because you're working alongside other people who love 'the thing' the way you love 'the thing'. You can get in that satisfying flow state and feel like you're where you were made to be and people *pay you for it*. What could be better?

THE CONS OF LIKING WHAT YOU DO

Be prepared to work with people who don't care about 'the thing' as much as you.

People who see it as a means to an end, or simply a way to make money, or don't see the fun in refining and improving the thing. People whose only interest is in packaging and maximising 'the thing', no matter the toll it takes on its quality. You will spend a lot of time trying not to resent them for this.

If you get to do the cool thing and you are not *also* required to do some uninspiring meetings and paperwork around the cool thing, you will be an anomaly. In all likelihood, *every* cool thing has paperwork attached (which is really only good news if your passion is paperwork and admin). The other potential hurdle is that to be able to 'progress' (translation: get paid fairly as your skill level rises), you will have to enter a management position. I've been a manager several times, and I'd like to take this moment to publicly apologise to everyone I have ever line-managed. The assumption was always that because I was good at the tasks I was doing day to day, I would also be good at teaching those skills and at building a system around other people doing those tasks. This, as it turns out, is a wildly false equivalence. 'Pedagogy' isn't a word I've always known, but anyone who is familiar with the concept will tell you that teaching is a separate skill. Some people have expertise at their job AND the flair for showing others *how* they do it, but they're generally the exceptions to the rule. Even though it's BS that 'those who can't do, teach', in my experience it is sometimes true that 'those who *can* do, shouldn't' . . . Well, at least in my case. Ditto the other skills of management: building systems, workflow negotiations, delegating with grace and mentoring with patience. They're all *new* skills, separate disciplines, HARD things to master. And just because you're adept at one, doesn't mean you've got a head start at the other.

This feels obvious when you apply it to some industries and it mysteriously needs spelling out in other fields. A good actor doesn't always make a good director. A great hairdresser doesn't automatically make a great small business owner. A talented painter doesn't make a talented gallery curator. A good pilot doesn't make a good air traffic controller. A good bartender doesn't make a good brewer . . . you get the idea.

On top of that, becoming a manager generally means you have to stop, or shrink the time you spend, doing 'the thing'. The thing you enjoyed in the first place. The thing you spent so long getting good at. It's sad! So, if you pick this option and you don't think you'd have a flair for teaching, or enjoy organising other people doing the skill as much as you enjoy actually doing the skill itself, you have three options. One: reconcile yourself to being on a similar wage to your starting salary for a long period of time, which means that you need to make sure it's enough for you to build the life you want. Two: start the cogs whirring on a plan to go freelance, either in the near or far-flung future. Infuriatingly, if you just want to get better at a specific skill, it's often easier to break away and charge a higher rate as a freelancer than it is to get a pay rise inhouse. Three: look at ways you can rebuild the structure of your industry, and flirt with the idea of disrupting the 'this is just the way things are done' mentality. This option is wonderful and possible; but it's also worth weighing up how much time organising a systemic mutiny will take away from your time doing 'the thing'. The short-term irony of missing out on using your original skill set in order to fight for the right to spend your career refining that skill set will probably be worth it, but it's good to think hard before you leap.

LIKE WHAT YOU'RE DOING IT FOR

This could involve working at a more formally organised force for good, like a charity or a non-profit or a cooperative – or maybe just a business that's trying to solve a problem the world needs fixing whilst causing as little harm as possible. In this kind of role, it's not so much about the skill set you already have (in most cases you can learn a skill that's needed), but about what your toil is working *towards*, where the fruits of your labour are being directed. Think Noah building the Ark: not his forte, but he learned on the job and got those animals marching in two by two (hurrah!).

THE PROS OF LIKING WHAT YOU DO YOUR JOB FOR

For some people, knowing that the fruits of their labour are contributing to something that they have a deep connection to brings an unmatched steadiness and purpose to even the most mundane of roles. Even the paperwork becomes a powerful act of resistance, the long hours go by faster, the little inconveniences are deemed worth it whenever they think of the big picture. This kind of purposeful resilience and drive is something we could all do with mastering, and apply to at least some part of our lives; whether that's partnership, parenting, or picking up the poo of a pet we love. Whether you want to flex this muscle in the workplace is up to you, but I think this one is the most steadfast option if you're looking for a really long-term vocation. My interest in a field or a skill might change over time, but if there's a wider narrative at play about why I'm doing it, it really helps.

I used to think my current work (mainly making video essays about social change, conscious consumption and the climate crisis) was in the first category, that I loved the act of doing it. But now, more days than not, I actually wonder if it sits more truthfully in the 'doing it FOR' category. I think there's something wonderful about the way LOVE of a thing can light a fire up someone's arse, but personally my ignition seems to be fanned AS well if not BETTER by . . . spite. Indignation. That feeling of knowing that the world is *so close* to being nice, and yet so sloppily run. That it's full of frustration and fear and spite and war and pointless spam emails and bad vegan cheese, when it needn't be. I have a suspicion that it's healthy to run off a little bit of fury, because the satisfaction will be all the stronger when you feel like you're winning.

Whatever your driving force, it doesn't need to make sense to anyone else; it just needs to put enough petrol in your tank to keep you bouncing out of bed each morning and feeling content at the end of the day as you head for home.

It's worth noting that this doesn't mean your work should be made up of tasks you hate. You don't have to *love* doing it, but you shouldn't *mind* doing it. Having a job that is your version of Jesus' Stations of the Cross isn't going to help anybody in the long term. The smugness of feeling as if you are self-sacrificing, that you're 'suffering' for a cause, can only fuel you for so long. You're likely to burn out or become a pretty insufferable colleague, cosmically negating any 'good' you think you might be doing in your role.

THE CONS OF LIKING WHAT YOU DO YOUR JOB FOR

There's nothing wrong with working for a cause, but it's very important to make sure that over the years you don't start to believe that the organisation that you've teamed up with to help that cause doesn't merge *with* the cause. Abandoning the role isn't the same as abandoning the cause (it's likely if you *really care,* you'll be unable to hand in your notice on caring, even if you wanted to).

It's also worth staying alert to signs your workplace is abandoning the cause that initially drew you to it. If they want a 'passion hire' they should be prepared to uphold the intentions that have inspired you to make the compromises we often must make to work in these roles: a lower pay packet, longer hours, very little budget to execute the impossible. I've noticed that the people we should be protecting the most are those most targeted by this kind of exploitation: care workers, teachers, nurses, the list could go on forever. It's important to check in with yourself and weigh up your impact against the toll it might be taking on your personal wellbeing, and be prepared to tweak and strategise, should push come to shove.

LIKE THE WAY YOU'RE DOING IT

The 'way' you do your job might refer to the location and environment you work in, the flexibility around when you do that work, or the volume of hours you have to work to make enough money to live off. Your 'way' might be the life the job allows you to have outside of working hours, whether that's enabling your chosen lifestyle, your passion project, side hustle or supporting those you love. Perhaps your real focus is travel, so working in short, intense bursts at something that is hard but very lucrative, and then taking an extended period off to explore the world, makes sense to you. Perhaps your focus is parenting, so taking a role that isn't ideal but gives you the flexibility and the funds to be able to be there when your kids come home takes priority. Maybe your passion is the Victorian art of glass-eye making, and you need a job that never requires you to work weekends so you can attend all the Glass-Eye Conventions your heart yearns for. Maybe you simply don't feel that strongly about anything yet, and would like some time to find out, or maybe you've been through something hard and are still getting to know yourself.

In this case, your priority is finding an industry or a workplace that has decent working conditions under late-stage capitalism. Godspeed, great warrior! I'm kidding: these places are few and far between but they do exist. It might be doing something that doesn't interest other people, or (if your life allows you) comes in the form of unusual work patterns or is located in a remote part of the country. With this kind of role, what you'll like about your job is what it allows you to do when you are not working, whether that's in the form of free time, flexible working or financial compensation.

THE PROS OF LIKING THE WAY YOU DO YOUR JOB

You're able to pursue other things that would have been harder to immerse yourself in, or even impossible, without said job. Whether it's working part-time and flexibly around homeschooling your children, or doing intense manual labour in the mountains for a few months that allows you to have a few months off to build a pirate ship in your back garden – a role like this allows you to call the shots more often outside of work hours.

You're likely to be able to weather workplace dramas more easily, since your focus might not be on perfecting your craft or rising in the ranks. You are able to think with a cooler head in a crisis at work, since the stakes are lower for you compared to someone who has a bone-deep passion for a project and can't see the wood for the trees. If you can nab a job where you can work in batches or seasons, somewhere that works in segments like terms, missions, projects or contracts (and compensates you well enough that you can take breaks between these times of intense work), you might find it suits your temperament better than working most calendar weeks of the year.

You might use that freedom to be able to hone your expertise without having to mould it into something that is commercially appealing. You might be able to spend your time healing from a hard past, or deepening the relationships in your life, or volunteering for a cause that would never be able to afford your help otherwise.

THE CONS OF LIKING THE WAY YOU DO YOUR JOB

If the 'way' you do your job is the only thing you like about doing your job but you don't like the tasks, or the people, or the purpose, you'll have to safeguard against that eventually wearing you down. You have to weigh up the extent to which your activities outside of work are able to fulfil you, and if that works for you long term. I've found that roles where I know that whatever effort I put in is making profit that is being funnelled towards something I'm actively against can wear my soul down. It's easy to underestimate how much subconscious effort it takes to shut out the parts of your brain that know unfortunate truths – it's a muscle that gets weaker with time, not stronger. If you work for someone you disagree with for too long, I've found that all victories start to have a sourness to them, or a kind of droop that makes the celebration less exciting. A certain wariness is required when picking a role like this, because it's ripe for short-term gain and long-term regret.

Having said all this, I must remind you:

You deserve all three!

We're working towards a world where there *will be* all three for everyone! But until we get there, it's okay to half-arse your definition of job satisfaction. You might even find that being realistic about what a job can give you, and looking for things like purpose and fulfilment outside of the workplace, might bring that world about faster.

Questions to ask yourself:

Is there a way my industry could be run fairly?

Do I agree with the premise of my industry?

Is it creating something that people need, and/or if duplicated, would it be possible for everyone to have it without the world collapsing?

How can I use my passions, skills and personal vendettas outside of my career?

HALF-ARSE WORKPLACE HABITS

To help you finalise your divorce from whole-hearted work addiction (or from the guilt that comes with failing to do so), here are some practical ways you can apply half-arse techniques in the workplace, whilst still keeping your plates spinning . . .

APPLY WHEN YOU CAN DO HALF

It's likely that you've heard of the famous study that found that women will usually only apply for jobs where they meet 100 per cent of the qualifications specified on the job listing, whereas men are willing to apply even if they only meet 60 per cent of the things on a prospective role's wish list.

This is usually held up as evidence either that men get promotions because of their arrogance, or that women pass up promotions because of a lack of self-belief.

If we dig deeper though, as the *Harvard Business Review* did, we can see that it's probably not a crisis of confidence; rather a crisis of obedience. The women they surveyed gave the reasons for why they didn't apply for those roles, and most fell under the banner of 'I didn't think I was allowed to/I thought I was following the guidelines by not applying'. It's not that they were being bashful, they were attempting to be accurate.

There seems to have been a miscommunication around etiquette, so let me set the record straight: it is not rude to apply for a job you are only half qualified for if you are also willing to wholeheartedly dedicate yourself to it.

Two reasons: the bar is lower than you think, and *actively wanting* to do the job is more of an asset than you realise.

This is a great example of why a transfer from an educational environment to a work environment can be confusing. Most of the time, in an exam or a test, you can't negotiate, charm or project yourself to a good grade with pure passion alone. In a great deal of jobs you most *definitely can* get places just by caring. So many job roles nowadays – with the obvious exception of high-stakes jobs in professions like medicine, military and science – rely on much more nebulous skills like patience, diplomacy and charisma. I have been on the other side of several hiring processes and it was incredibly eye opening.

Very few candidates met all of the criteria (the list can be very long and a little arbitrary). With those who did, when it came to the interview stage it became clear that while they *technically* had done the tasks on the list before, they weren't very excited to work on the projects that the job entailed, or very curious about the other humans they'd be working alongside. On the flip side, some of the candidates who on paper didn't tick all the boxes, brought energy and kindness and curiosity into the interview room with them. Their considered attention and enthusiasm was infectious: it sounds cheesy, but most true things are. They'd often end up being hired because they didn't seem like they'd be careless in their tasks, even if they were new to them; that they would be thoughtful and consistent and likely (because they were genuinely interested in the role) to stay longer.

You might picture yourself up against an elite class of skilled professionals who are all better than you. That could be true, but even if it were, it doesn't mean that they will want the job should they be offered it. If they're as good as you have conjured in your mind, won't they be in high demand? Likely interviewing for other roles too? If you don't apply, you're only guaranteeing that you won't be second, or third, or fourth in line, ready to take the job when the cool kids go 'nah, thanks but no thanks'.

It's also important to remember that however unbiased those doing the hiring should be, they're also hiring someone that they will then have to hang out with every day, longer than they might get to spend with their family or friends. I would personally much rather hang out with someone who was still learning but happy to be there, rather than someone who was incredibly talented but didn't give two hoots. So, if you see a job listing for a role that genuinely excites you and you can show it, in the eyes of the interviewer you're already halfway there.

WORKPLACE SPY

Of all places, imposter syndrome shouldn't be something that affects us in the workplace, since we've specifically been *hired* to be there. Not only should you be in the room, someone else wants you in the room so much that they're *paying you to be in it*. That's all great in theory, but I know the 'practice' is another ball game entirely. I have spent a lot of my working life with the phrase *'they're going to find out that you're shit'* playing on repeat in the back of my head during meetings.

Do you know what fixed it for me?

No, it wasn't morning mantras of girlbossing phrases like 'I am a champion' that brainwashed me into believing in myself. It was the realisation that if I was in fact 'shit', that wasn't really my problem.

Even if I didn't always believe in my own skill, I usually thought the people above me were professionals, with professional clout. *They* had hired me. *They* continued to let me work there. I knew that I was doing the best job I could, with the resources and the skills I had. If it was bad, it was up to *them* to let me know, not for me to guess. It was up to them to help me improve, train me, give me helpful feedback. IF I was terrible, and no one had found out yet, did that make me an imposter, or did that make me something cooler?

Didn't that make me a *super spy*?

It might be silly, but it was a great re-framing of my doubts. Instead of building myself up as 'the best employee ever', on the days when I doubted myself, I decided that I wasn't the worst worker, but *the best spy*. I had fooled the experts. I continued to do a mediocre job and no one had clocked me. That, in a backwards way, was a pretty impressive skill, right?

A good spy keeps notes, so I did. I filed useful emails with piles of information in a folder called 'spy material', and if I ever needed to know something important, I'd go and forage there for answers. Not to shamefully unearth something I 'should already know'. No. I dug to find the tips that would help me convince the powers that be that I knew what I was doing.

By proxy, I started to *actually* know what I was doing, without my panic putting me in freeze mode. I tricked myself into self-belief. I kept a document of any praise I received, or stats that showed my progress or impact on a project – not as a cringey, smug self-congratulatory back rub for myself, but as good evidence to pass on to . . . whoever I was spying for. Charlie? Judi Dench? I never got that far with the fantasy, but apparently I didn't need to, it worked anyway.

Being a 'spy' who takes notes can also take the form of workplace advocacy, or as I like to call it, intentional eavesdropping. I once worked in a professional environment that attracted what my mum might call 'characters'. I didn't stay long, but for the time I was there I overheard some strange workplace conversations that definitely might have warranted an HR meeting. One time I overheard a superior sitting on the next bank of desks who was speaking to one of my colleagues in a way that could have filled a bingo card of inappropriate euphemisms: a smattering of racism, a swirl of general rudeness and a dollop of sexism to top it all off. While a public display of indignation might have won me 'allyship points', I was also acutely aware of embarrassing my colleague or taking the agency away from her to respond on her own terms. Perhaps in a social setting I might have reacted differently, but employment is incredibly personal and high stakes. I didn't want to cast myself in the role of 'saviour' whilst also jeopardising her position further. Instead, I pulled up a blank document on my computer and transcribed the conversation they were having, word for word. I then discreetly sent her an email, outlining that I thought the interaction was inappropriate, attached the transcript with my signature at the bottom and told her that I'd be happy to be a witness or support should she want to make a complaint.

I wish I had more examples like that one, but in truth I was useless more often than I was useful. My point isn't that I'm a model colleague or that that example will be universally applicable; it's only to make the point that advocating for the people around you doesn't have to take up a lot of time and you don't have to be an expert to start. Thinking about small, subtle, spy-like ways you can underline any points of friction that you spot, and making sure you already have a few ideas in your mind of how to respectfully respond when they arise, is spy-for-change energy. If in doubt, create spaces for people to talk, be the listener before the leader. Half is more than most people are giving in this instance.

DON'T BE AFRAID TO BE SEEN HALF-ARSING

Do you know that feeling when you've been seeing and experiencing something your whole life but then you're given a new phrase to reframe it and it totally changes how you see it? I recently learned the term 'WAGE THEFT' and it's turned my little world upside down. Wage theft is when an employer fails to pay wages or give employee benefits that have been agreed in a contract. This can come in the form of failing to give the correct amount of paid holiday, sick or parental leave, but more commonly it's the failure to pay workers for their overtime. From staying late to working through your lunch break, overtime was normalised in every work environment I've ever been in.

The *Big Issue* estimates that wage theft amounts to £26 billion in the UK alone every year, which is around £7,200 per person.

Wanting to work overtime is easy to understand, I've done it myself for at least the past decade. You want to seem helpful and dedicated, especially if you're new or early in your career. You want to reduce short-term friction with your colleagues by getting everything done, even if you've been assigned more than is humanly possible within your legal working hours. You want to do your future self a favour by protecting them from the consequences of failing to complete everything.

But I've recently started realising the long-term downsides to overtime: by completing what should be impossible (because it is, within your normal hours), you raise the expectations of your workload going forward; you completed it this week, so why shouldn't you next week? You cover the tracks of poor management, who have incorrectly allocated workloads and perhaps over-promised their superiors, based on the assumption that you will work for free. **You've artificially raised the expectations for your department or your role,** so that the next person who has your job will be expected to do the same exploitative hours that you have done; except when it's their time, they won't have a choice.

Self-sabotage is a weird thing; I'm often much more willing to screw myself over, than I am able to bear the thought of indirectly screwing over future people who sit at my desk. And so I recommend the following policies to any chronic over-arsers out there:

1. Have somewhere to be.

For at least some of your contracted days, schedule something in your diary after work that has some kind of external accountability built in: just like a nursery pick up or the school run. Book an afterwork drink, even if it's just for an hour, especially if other friends also struggle to leave on time. You can call them 'overwork accountability pints' or 'anti-wage theft hour' – with full permission for your friends to call you or give you a forfeit if you're late. Join clubs, book classes. Or, if you're done with human interaction by 5 p.m., book a solo cinema screening that's non-refundable or a swimming slot, calendar block in a bath. Anything that reminds your brain that you contractually have a cut-off point after which you're allowed to be a non-working human again.

2. Tot up your over-trying.

Sit down and calculate (truthfully) how many overtime hours you think you do in a month. I'm not asking you to go cold turkey and stop completely, but *halve* that number and make a list of other places in your life that would be transformed if you were to give that time to them. Perhaps it's a frazzled friend who could do with a hand, or a community garden that could use just two hours a month of your digging power, or a charity that could use some pro bono hours of your expertise. Imagine how good you could get at the recorder, or puppet ventriloquy, or underwater hockey, if you allowed yourself to spend those hours practising them. Make it known in your workplace what your out-of-hours passion is, mention it in passing, show them pictures, share the joy. You'll make it feel okay for them to do the same, and have them rooting for you when you are trying to leave on time.

3. Remember that 100 per cent is not lazy.

Remind yourself that refusing to do more than your contracted hours isn't half-arsing; you're doing 100 per cent of what you promised you would. Staying later is giving *more* than your full commitment, at the price of other important things. Be aware of self-talk that uses words like 'lazy', 'behind', 'apathetic': by giving your all while you're at work and leaving on time, you're giving yourself your best chance of staying healthy, balanced and, as a nice side effect, becoming a better employee. I don't know if you've ever worked with someone who is burned out, frazzled and ill-rested . . . but that's not the kind of colleague any of us deserve!

There has been a lot of discussion around the trend of 'quiet quitting' in recent years. Its critics define it as reducing the effort you put into your job, but not by so much that you get fired. Those who are pro quiet quitting define it as simply doing what you are contracted to do, to the best of your ability, but quitting the idea of going 'above and beyond' if it's to the detriment of your own health. The second definition sounds perfectly reasonable to me. So much so that I wonder if it is weird to call it 'quitting' at all. That we can make ourselves feel as if not giving away our time as a mandatory 'freebie' to our employer is equivalent to quitting altogether shows us what a chokehold capitalism has on our sense of balance and reality.

HALF-ARSERS ARE UNION MEMBERS

This one is definitely a 'do as I say, not as I did' moment. When I was working in a more traditional workplace, on a bank of desks with an employment contract and a branded mug, I spent an awful lot of time advocating for myself. It ultimately resulted in me job-hopping almost every year or so, as it was usually the best way to secure realistic work hours, pay rises or the creative freedom I longed for. Looking back, I really wish I'd spent the small amount of energy I had left on trying to change some of the structures that kept my requests at bay. Only one of the five office workplaces I frequented had a union, but I should have joined it. Now my work is more nebulous and 'multi-hyphenate', unions are fewer and far between, but I've joined the ones relevant to me and am resolved to be as active as I can.

It's the 'quiet quitting' trend, but with a layer of purpose and strategy.

It might require a bit of effort, but in the long term I'd wager it's much less effort to fight alongside your colleagues than it would be for each of you to do the work of negotiating behind closed doors. You can compare notes, share resources, tap into a hive mind, build trust. It will also save you the spiritual labour of all having to needlessly job hop annually. The inefficiency of building great team dynamics and workflow only to have an industry re-jig every few years is a little silly – I think we'd all be able to stop exhausting ourselves if we were able to build long-term, fair working conditions for all. Half-arsing en masse is how things change long term.

KNOW WHEN YOU'RE HALF WAY

I know it doesn't seem like it now, but you *will* get really good at what you do. Even if you don't specialise and become what the world needs more of, a 'jack of all trades', you will become more mature, more able to spot patterns and react wisely and just generally very, very *useful*.

Before you get to that point, it's a good idea to revisit that Venn diagram of possible job satisfaction: liking what you do, liking why you do it or liking the way you get it done. If you have one of those gems, which is the next best one you'd like? Now you have some more skills to barter with, more leverage, might it be possible to get two out of three? Might it, in your wildest dreams, be in any way feasible to get all three?

It's understandable and often unavoidable to work for a company that you disagree with, especially at the beginning of your career. After a while, some of us get lucky; we have the chance to bundle up what we've learned and run for the hills. We have windows of opportunity in which the curtains flutter and give us a glimpse of those ways our work could be used for something better. Or, at least, something more neutral.

The tragedy is that many people don't spot the opportunity to turn off at the next exit, or they don't think they're 'good' enough to jump 'just yet'. They wait to be the expert, the best, the perfect employee, even if they waste decades in doing so. They picture their 'out' being the off-chance of a lottery win, or a suddenly wealthy spouse, or the death of a millionaire relative they didn't know they had.

The escape hatch might not come in the form of wealth. Sometimes it comes in the form of a weird new project you hear about through the grapevine. It knocks as a quitting colleague who is willing to show you how they escaped. It descends as an offer of a pay rise that you turn down in exchange for a reduction in hours for the same pay, so you can side-hustle your way to something better. It calls in the form of a night class, or an unusual article, or a midnight hunch.

There are workplaces that have a rotten way of working, a rotten model for day-to-day stuff, but that are working towards something great. There are those that have a great way of doing things but are creating something that won't benefit the world, or the money at the top gets tucked away somewhere awful. Which category of rotten your workplace is, and how resilient you are, will determine how long you can stand to stay. It won't all depend on you, at certain intervals there will be external forces that keep you from jailbreaking; but you must be on the lookout for an exit sign, and believe that it will appear eventually. It's Gatsby's green light, but for the late-stage capitalist worker.

For me, the green light appeared once when I realised there was an opening to ask for a pay rise, but I asked for a reduction in hours instead. I used my extra day, and then two, to build my own workplace from my sofa. The second time the green light appeared, it was after my partner and I had been sitting in our tiny, very expensive capital city flat for almost a year during a pandemic. We both realised that, despite our previous hesitations, we had a feeling that the loss of London might be worth bearing in exchange for a chance out of our office jobs, and a chance to live a more financially stable existence. We could not afford freelance life in London; but elsewhere, perhaps where I grew up in the Midlands, it might feasibly hold us up. We were in equal parts daring and lucky; it worked.

When I quit my job, I wasn't an expert. I wasn't a manager or a boss or a prodigy. But, I estimated, over the years I had been working, I had become about halfway as competent as I had the potential to be. If I devoted that same amount of time again to perfecting my craft, I thought I'd be confident in saying 'yeah, I'm pretty good at this'. But I reasoned that, by the time that happened, I would have contributed a lot to a collection of companies that didn't entirely align with what I thought was most important, or urgent, or interesting to do. I'd have taught their workforce, improved their systems, I'd have undoubtedly added to their wins and to their bottom line. Unless the culture changed drastically overnight, I would have inevitably worked hundreds of hours of unpaid overtime (sorry: *wage theft*). I tried to picture that future self, a decade or so ahead. Was she happy? Was she being treated fairly? Did she feel like the right people were reaping the rewards of the hard work she had sowed?

The shift to elsewhere might seem either very brave or very silly. If you succeed they'll call it the former, but first they'll call you the latter. But you must do it; you must run before whatever is rotting sinks into your bones. And do it before you're the best; do it when, by your estimation, you're halfway there.

IN DEFENCE OF THE SIDE-HUSTLE

Like with most topics in the 'zeitgeist', the side-hustle has often been presented as something new and scary, drumming up either extreme excitement or extreme panic. Will the side-hustle destroy what little work–life balance the modern world has to offer? Is it a fresh signifier of widespread greed or desperate lack of financial resources? Is it a symptom of a toxic society addicted to productivity? Is it simply 'What Ambitious People Do'? If you don't have one, do you lack ambition? Are the side-hustlers of today the future leaders of tomorrow?

What is often missed in this debate is that having one single source of income that you spend a large chunk of set hours earning per week was not the norm for most of human history, nor is it now for much of the world. I think to warn so strongly against taking on *any* extra projects, however financially or spiritually fruitful, is to encourage an over-dependence on a single workplace to provide us with everything we might need out of life, from stability to fulfilment.

The problem with side-hustles isn't their existence in themselves, but the logistical nightmare of trying to experiment and build new systems alongside a modern workplace that demands so much of us. However, if we've mastered the steps of Half-Arse Workplace Habits, we should be able to reclaim the possibility of the half-arse side-hustle as a subversive force rather than a destructive one.

What I think is magical about the side-hustle is its capacity for positive half-arsing. You aren't throwing ALL your time, ALL your money or ALL of your hopes into it. It's only half *at most*. You don't have to claim to be an expert to start something on the side, and others won't expect that of you. You only need to be half-good at it, and to be brave enough to be seen trying.

We often imagine side-hustles to be 'half-arse' versions of 'real' jobs. And this can be the case: you could be developing a genuinely effective skincare ingredient that is going to take the cosmetics world by storm, or coding a new social media platform to rival the ones run by awful rich men (yes please) . . . but world domination doesn't have to be your end goal. Your side-hustle doesn't have to be expandable and profitable to be worth doing. That doesn't relegate it to the mere realm of 'hobby'. A hobby is simply the practice of doing an activity, semi-regularly; a side-hustle is about building something that you would like to exist, but doesn't already. For example, a hobby might be playing football on a local team at the weekend. A side-hustle would be starting your own amateur league. Taking a course of bass guitar lessons is a hobby. Starting a reggae-meets-folktronica band and playing the local craft fete circuit is a strong side-hustle. Occasionally attempting to grow string beans in your garden is a great hobby. Reclaiming some land in your area to start a community garden is a side-hustle.

If we can assuage some of the possible toxic pitfalls of the half-arsed side-hustle, I am confident that we have more to gain than we have to lose. Here are some ways in which a strategic side-hustle could be a great addition to your life . . .

CHILDHOOD DREAMS ON YOUR OWN TERMS

If you once dreamed of a career then, as soon as you learned its pitfalls thought 'I can't be arsed with this . . .' then side-hustling could be a great way to avoid parting with your passion, even if the industry that has grown up around it isn't for you. From the age of about twelve ALL I wanted was to be a musical performer in the West End. It's what I spent my evenings and weekends training for, it's what my journals were full of, it dictated all of my academic choices up until I left school at eighteen. I sat out of university applications because I knew where I would be . . . on the stage! Except, when I got into a summer school at a prestigious London drama school, two weeks was all I needed to realise that the pay-off of actually becoming a musical performer was not worth the life I would be required to lead in order to get what I wanted. The industry was much more cutthroat than I had imagined, the conditions cruel, the financial subsidies needed to stay afloat near impossible if you didn't already come from wealth. With a heavy heart I looked for a more feasibly joyful way to live my life, and turned my back on the red curtains. Cue the tiny violins.

It's a particular tragedy of the arts that if we don't find our place in the 'industry' surrounding them, we're automatically demoted to being simple consumers. It's often seen as 'cringe' to continue to participate in creating art, of any kind, if no one is willing to pay you. It wasn't until I was in my thirties that it occurred to me that I was *allowed* to do it for fun. That, even if I wasn't that talented, it wasn't a *crime* to do it anyway. When I moved to a new town and saw that the local theatre was running auditions for one of my favourite musicals, I pushed down the squirming feeling of being an imposter and showed up to read for a part. Being part of that cast healed a little part of my teenage self that I didn't know had shrivelled inside me. Even though our costumes were homemade, our set sparse, our voices occasionally cracking and the run only ten nights long . . . I realised that I had been making myself feel embarrassed for 'failing at theatre' when really I'd only 'failed' to make it profitable. There was a huge, gaping difference.

RECLAIM THE JACK OF ALL TRADES

When you call someone a 'jack of all trades', everyone hears the silent echo of the rest of the sentence:

'A jack of all trades is a master of none.'

It's used as a shorthand to imply that someone can do a little bit of everything, but *nothing* very well. It's a lightly disguised insult: jacks of all trades do bodge jobs, they're guessing, they have chosen breadth over depth, they haven't reached their potential and they probably never will.

What if I told you that that wasn't the end of the rhyme?

'A jack of all trades is a master of none,
But oftentimes better than a master of one.'

I KNOW. I spent most of my twenties using that phrase as a bar to beat myself over my head with. As someone who tended to 'job-hop' every year or so, I was worried that I might not ever settle and become really 'good' at something. As it turns out, that became my 'superpower', for want of a better phrase. After a few years of doing this, being a 'multi-hyphenate' – not only having worked across adjacent departments and industries, but also having a string of side-hustles that informed my full-time job – became *the reason* I was hired for roles. Eventually, it gave me the skills I needed to set up my own small business and fuse my seemingly fragmented knowledge into one coherent little machine.

These 'amateur' projects, I think, might be our natural human instinct to make associations and create connections in a world where we are pressured to specialise, to sink all of our waking hours into one thing and to pretend that it's going to advance our world and/or be incredibly interesting. Some people *are* wired to be experts and thank goodness; we need them. Far more of us, I fear, are being prevented from fully inhabiting our most natural, wonderful state: pottering about. Sampling different things. Playing.

YOU MIGHT END UP MAKING A JOB OUT OF IT ANYWAY

The world of work has never been so weird or been changing so fast. What might be a wonderful, completely unprofitable experiment this decade, may well be a viable career in the next one. In 2009 I started uploading my book reviews and video essays to a fairly new website called YouTube, which was 50 per cent illegally uploaded pirated movies, 40 per cent cat videos and then a very small community of early vloggers uploading their thoughts onto grainy webcams from bedrooms across the world. This website, which had no revenue avenues, barely any coverage and was seen to be a quirky, borderline creepy hobby, became my full-time job eleven years later.

While your peripheral, niche passion might always be just that, we have no business trying to predict the way the world or work will go in the next few decades. Imagine the boiling fury you might feel for denying yourself the space to explore new ways of creating, or remoulding a field that interests you . . . only in ten years to have to watch others make it their full-time gig.

I also think it's good to consider what you are telling YOU if you deny yourself the joy of working on what genuinely interests you based on whether others around you value it, or what its 'market value' is. To not pursue it at all, even in small chunks throughout your life, is by proxy agreeing with the sceptics. So whether you're evangelical about pirate-metal or hand-carved clog making, you owe yourself at least a little half-arsing at it, now and again.

At the end of the day, a job is an 'occupation' and you might not be able to control the amount of time it occupies you for. You have, however, the half-arse permission from me to twiddle with the dials that determine how much real estate that occupation takes up in your heart. You are the childminder of your imagination, so don't just put a metaphorical iPad (AKA a busy career) in its hands. A little mischief is encouraged. There are so many ways to be occupied in this world, ways to be full and present and to tweak your small corner of it to your liking, if only you can be arsed to look.

Was that your belly rumbling or mine? Time for lunch, I think . . .

Half-Arse Vegan*

(meat-eaters welcome)

If the road to hell is paved with good intentions, then the road to a liveable planet is built with the cobblestones of half-arsers trying their best. If you've ever felt like overhauling your personal lifestyle habits in pursuit of what you've heard is '#sustainable', you'll know what a moral minefield it can be.

Raking through every eco-choice, from flying to recycling to driving, would take a whole library of thoughts to do thoroughly. Since we're half-arsers here, I'm going to pick one traditionally 'eco-warrior' topic to get stuck into, in the hopes that it will make your brain spark and sizzle with ideas on how these principles could apply to other aspects of your life that could be 'sustainably spiced up'. The question of whether animal products have a place on my plate (and if eschewing them will EVEN MAKE A DIFFERENCE) perfectly embodies the common conundrums we face as we try to make choices in a world where the floor is made of lava but the cheese sandwiches are made of yum.

Don't worry! I'm not going to unravel a scroll and read to you all the reasons you should be a vegan.

Until I was thirty years old, I ate meat with wild abandon.

At the time of writing, that's close to 90 per cent of my life. My high horse bolted long ago (and good on him I say, I wish him well) so don't worry; I'm not going to sit here and dangle my puny three-year record in front of you like a tiny golden ticket to saintdom.

There are lots of places to get your questions answered, straighten your facts and have that 'lightbulb' moment. Mine came after reading *We Are the Weather* by Jonathan Safran Foer, but yours might come from watching a documentary, a chance chat over coffee or even a life-changing slice of vegan cheesecake.

This chapter is for those of us (and we're increasing in number every day) that know the headline reasons why we can't keep eating the way we've been eating . . . but can't seem to shimmy that *hunch* into *action*. It's also for anyone who, for whatever reason, knows they won't be able to 'go the whole hog' (ahem) and give up animal products entirely.

We're sold on the facts, we can hear the music, but getting up to dance feels impossible. Overwhelming. Possibly even pointless.

Perhaps we're nervous about completely changing our food habits after a lifetime battling self-imposed rules around food.

Perhaps we aren't sure if we can beat our impulses every time, and don't want to risk being a hypocrite if we slip up.

It could be that we have a specific food in mind that would break our heart to part with – or a specific meal that's significant to us (*that* food from Diwali, Easter, Ramadan, Hanukkah or Christmas, or even just a good old Sunday roast).

Maybe you live somewhere where there aren't a whole lot of vegan alternatives in your supermarket, or where asking for a vegan menu at your local pub would get you laughed out of the door. Perhaps you have a list of Very Awkward Food Allergies™ that the world doesn't accommodate and you can't bear to strike *even more* yummy things off the list.

They're all very reasonable concerns to have. I would have been suspicious of both my own motives and yours if, after one lecture on veganism, we'd converted to devout plant-munchers overnight. The powers of self-preservation run in all of our veins; thanks to millennia of natural selection, we're all the great[100] grandchildren of the most cautious people in the village.

It's good to chat it over. Research yourself. Have a think.

When I think of the phrase 'the vegan debate', an image of a shouty chat-show row pops into my head: a ruddy-faced man muttering to himself about the sacred nature of his sausage versus an activist with good intentions but very little charisma. It is an unfair, inaccurate picture for my subconscious to conjure, since so much of the debate at any given moment isn't going on between two people on national television. Most of the time we're having it privately; with ourselves.

In this chapter we'll mull over some of the reasons you might be on the fence about veganism, or similar eco-friendly life choices, and why you have the green light (from me, at least) to absolutely half-arse it. It's also an interesting basis from which to inspect 'half-arsing' from a moral perspective, to explain why it's not the same thing as 'laziness', 'indifference' or 'being rubbish'. If, by the end of our chat, you're willing to give it half an arse, we'll come up with a plan of how to make it (half) happen.

FINGER-POINTING IS BORING: FROM BLAME TO RESPONSIBILITY

Food is personal. At the beginning of our life, the people who choose and give us food are our most intimate providers. Learning to feed ourselves is one of the first accomplishments we're praised for. One of our first character markers is our favourite food. Before we can even speak, in that period of our lives where our guardians are obsessed with us but haven't got many clues about our personality, what we devour and what we reject becomes the first preferences that make us 'us'.

We don't really know what Donny is going to be like as a person but we SURE KNOW that he hates carrots! What a little maverick!

As we start to self-describe, what we love to eat is one of the things we're taught to reel off about ourselves:

My name is Leena!
I'm five and three quarters!
My favourite colour is purple!
My favourite food is pancakes!

It's no wonder any critique of our food choices feels like someone is peeking around our bedroom door and critiquing the way we make our bed. GET OUT!

If we didn't grow up in poverty ourselves, the first time we hear about 'poor people' is probably at the dinner table.

Some children don't get ANY food for their dinner! Now simmer down and eat your chicken nuggets.

Food becomes a signifier of culture, of care, of tradition and of comfort. For me, occasions were inextricable from the food we ate during them, becoming sacred with their repetition: greasy chips after a swimming lesson; a gammon joint on a Sunday; ice cream on holiday; cream pastries to commemorate the birthday of a dead relative. (My mum invented this family tradition and while I don't think her motives were completely pure, I have to respect the sweet-tooth hustle. The excuses for this ritual also multiply over time. GENIUS. It really did teach me a great life lesson: that grief is served best with whipped cream.)

I added to the traditions as I became an adult; bacon sandwiches for a hangover, slabs of chocolate for a painful period, baked camembert for a breakup.

These rituals formed the glue that held together the moments I lived through. The thought that they could be 'wrong' tugged at buried things I wasn't ready to uproot: what my parents taught me was safe, what my primary school taught me was balanced, what my tastebuds taught me was delicious. They couldn't all be wrong, could they? They were the tectonic plates of my life, and if they shifted, what was I supposed to stand on? What else was a lie?

I knew about veganism for well over a decade before I darkened its door and chanced a toe over the threshold. Most of us do. I saw PETA protests on TV, was handed leaflets in the street by animal rights activists, I stumbled across YouTube videos of factory farm abuse . . . and I didn't engage with any of it, I simply walked or scrolled past.

I think there's a self-selection process when it comes to the types of vegans you are likely to run into if you didn't already grow up around them. Those who have been doing it the longest are usually the most vocal. In all likelihood, they've been doing it SO long that they've forgotten the emotional impact of hearing the information they're trying to impart. What probably came off as apathy from me was actually bottled panic. *If* they were right, there would be some pretty sobering repercussions for my fragile sense of self.

Could I be doing something *bad*? Not just on one occasion, but something I did every day? *Multiple times a day*? Was I a mug to believe what I'd been told? Has the world been making a fool of me? If so, what else have I been so easily tricked by? If I start researching this, and it turns out to be true, am I going to have to change the things that make me *me*? That make my family *us*? Am I going to have to scrap all these rituals that give my life rhythm? Am I going to have to defend something I barely understand every time I order a meal in front of other people?

What is strange about the right/wrong dichotomy is that so often we (especially in the Western world) have been taught to view righteousness as an individual pursuit, with an individual outcome.

Do something bad? Fail to change your ways? Enjoy your curse/jail time/eternal shift in hell!

Generally, the diagnosis of whether you are a 'good' or 'bad' egg is determined by your choices. Even though we rarely consider whether those 'choices' are yours to make: whether you have any political sway over the way your food system is run, whether logistically it is possible for you to fact check every aspect of the world you have grown up in.

The first bit of good news is that, when it comes to blame, I don't think I want to lay any of it on you. Or on myself. Convenient, I know, but I can back it up.

• On top of the huge marketing budgets behind your favourite chocolate, fast food and kitchen-cupboard-staple brands, there have been other powers influencing how you eat. Over decades industry lobbyists and meat-enthusiast investors have pumped billions into advertising campaigns like 'Got Milk', 'We Eat Balanced' and 'Beef – It's What's for Dinner' (paid for, respectively, by the California Milk Processor Board, the Agriculture and Horticulture

Development Board, which is funded by farmers, and the Beef Industry Council). These lessons even infiltrated your curriculum: remember those food pyramids and plate diagrams that always included lots of dairy and meat? If you weren't an expert on food production or nutrition at FIVE YEARS OLD, *how* were you supposed to know?

- It's likely that your government has invested a lot of money into making sure you keep eating meat and dairy products. For example, the EU spends 20 per cent of its entire annual budget (£24 billion) on subsidising animal farming. A whopping 90 per cent of a British grazing animal farmer's profits come from government subsidies.

- GPs aren't usually thoroughly trained to apply what we know about diet to patients' real lives and aren't required to update their knowledge after finishing medical school. One study in 2021 found that medical students in the UK and US were only given an average of eleven hours of nutrition training over the course of their whole education. Dr Michael Mosley, who presented the BBC's *Trust Me I'm a Doctor* before his tragic death in the summer of 2024, said that he learned 'almost nothing about nutrition' at medical school. We're all in need of a real re-education, and if even *doctors* are not up-to-date, can't we give ourselves a break?

- There is a false equivalence in some circles of activism that gives a bad faith reading to 'choices' that are actually just unexamined habits we have been taught by the world not to question. I don't think unknowingly funding abuse is the same as actually abusing someone. When we treat acts of consumerism as acts of direct malice, we start to construct a world in which the majority of people are *intentionally* causing harm rather than passively accepting it. Both are damaging, but intent matters. It matters because if we look out of our window and only see crowds of people who are selfish monsters, then trying to change the status quo seems like a hefty, undoable task. If we look out and see (I think more accurately) crowds of people who, given the right information, resources and opportunity, will do the least harmful thing (especially if it is made easy) . . . change seems within reach.

Even if you are a vegan and you think the main focus of our strategy *should* be shame, I honestly don't think the 'shoulds' matter as much as what will, in reality, work. Not because I'm not willing to hear your argument, but because *if* our objective is to save individual animals and the planet at large from impending doom, the priority can't be 'being technically correct' – call me fussy, but it must also ACTUALLY WORK.

As it turns out, shame is a really ineffective way of inspiring humans to pivot their behaviour. Anyone who has been on the wrong end of abuse hurled by a PE teacher from across a field in the pouring rain will know this, but if you need further evidence, Brené Brown has made a whole career out of clinically proving it. Our deer-brains get caught up in the headlights of it all and we end up either freezing or running away into the night.

It brings to mind the dilemma in Bertolt Brecht's *The Caucasian Chalk Circle* (based on the biblical judgement of King Solomon). Two women who both claim to be the mother of a baby are told to resolve the fight by taking an arm each and pulling the baby out of a chalk circle drawn around them on the floor. First over the line wins parental rights.

Except it is, of course, a trick; the woman who refuses to enter into the duel wins custody, because she doesn't want to hurt the baby by pulling on its arms until it rips in two. She would rather give the baby up than see it hurt.

It's the same with perfectionism when it comes to eating vegan; I don't think the sheep have a big preference for *who* stops eating meat, why they do it or how us hare-brained humans split the general reduction between us. They would just like to not die, please and thank you. Or, you know, baa-ram-ewe.

In fact, the Climate Change Committee (the experts appointed to advise our government on all things climate) are in agreement with the sheep. Their targets for Britain are a 20 per cent reduction in meat and dairy consumption by 2030 and a 35 per cent reduction for meat by 2050. NOTE: that is not *per person*; that's overall. If the experts are setting team-game goals, then what business have we pointing fingers? Instead, we could be busy cooking delicious meals for our friends, chomping down on dairy-free doughnuts and getting that percentage down, one meal at a time. I know which team I'd rather be on.

And so the second bit of good news is that while blame is something that cuts you off from other people, here the responsibility is a **team effort**. While I don't think it's necessary to accept blame for the way our food system has been set up, now we know how it works, we have a responsibility to work out where the wiggle room is to change things and . . . get wiggling!

THE THREE FOOD FIGHTS (AND HOW TO SURVIVE THEM)

We all get a bit tangled in the weeds when discussing this topic, don't we? Often I think it's because we're mashing our baked beans in with our chocolate sauce; that is to say, we're mixing what shouldn't be mixed.

The arguments for veganism can be split onto three plates:

Personal Health
Ethical
Ecological

This is all sounding far too school-y though, so I'd like to use my rough translations of these terms, for the sake of the next few pages:

~~Personal Health~~ Savvy
~~Ethical~~ Right
~~Ecological~~ Sensible

I like these shorthands because I'm less desensitised to them, and I think they boil the formality out of what should be very straightforward conversations.

It's *savvy* to watch out for your personal health, without getting swept up in overly dramatic anxieties around small possibilities of peril or finding yourself knee-deep in a Wikipedia hole surrounded by the treacle of un-cited stats and incomplete research.

It's *right* to care about living things that might not look like us, but throw tantrums, nuzzle their crushes and rearrange their bedding until it's *just* right, just like us.

It's *sensible* to keep an eye on who is looking after the floor you live on, and be able to tell when they're fobbing you off.

I have noticed that these conversations get tangled when one person starts to talk about what might or might not be *sensible* about a vegan diet, and then another retorts with a point about what is *right* to eat. A third offers an anecdote about how they read an article about how it wasn't very *savvy*, and that their cousin's friend's neighbour's postman had got sick when they tried it.

The first person gives an eye roll and starts muttering about how mass animal agriculture is pumping too many cow farts (methane) into the atmosphere. Then there's a squabble about gentrifying job opportunities and what will happen to the farmers, and then everyone feels embarrassed that they don't know what *would* happen to the farmers and gradually the debate descends into a squabble, or the suggestion of another round of drinks, and a pointed change of subject.

Communication disintegrates because while they're all talking about the same outcome (eating vegan) they're all talking about different parts of the debate. No one was willing to follow one of the arguments through to a conclusion, they just jumped between different topics. It effectively bungs up a route to an answer by saying 'it doesn't matter if your statement is true, because *if it is true*, we won't be able to action it because of The Farmers/Our vitamin needs/Our traditions/etc. – so really, it's best to not know.'

It's effectively like refusing to debate whether the car you're about to road trip in is safe enough to drive you across the country because if it's not, 'how are we going to move all our luggage to a different car, we'll never get a replacement in time, I'll be heartbroken because this is my favourite car and I've just changed the air freshener to a really expensive piña colada one!'

We can't establish whether the problem is solvable and hash out the details if we can't spend a little time objectively thinking about whether the problem even exists.

Or, in this analogy:

If the car is the earth, and the destination is the next 100 years, we really need to check if the clutch is going to fly off halfway through the Snowdonian mountains and send us into an icy Welsh lake. Piña colada air freshener or no Piña colada air freshener.

I've found making sure we agree which discussion we're in, and trying to stay on topic, means everyone stays better friends. Sometimes you even start to understand each other. Putting one concern on pause, for the length of one conversation, is well worth it if we're going to get to the bottom of things. And they end up leading into each other eventually anyway.

For example, if, as it turns out, not eating dairy, eggs and meat is very bad for the health of humans, then that changes whether killing animals to eat them for *survival* is right or wrong. If, as it turns out, eating animals is likely to directly or indirectly destroy the floor we live on and the air we breathe, making life itself impossible, that changes the discussion around it (hypothetically) being slightly worse for our health. Because, I hear, death is also really bad for your health.

When I say I'm a 'half-arse' vegan, I'm deciding that my main focus is on being *sensible*.

It means that I'm not claiming that my choices are *savvy* or *right* but that I'm starting with sensible and working my way up.

For the planet and the future, eating *as close* to a vegan diet as possible seems just . . . sensible? Not noble, not holier than thou, not valiant just . . . sensible.

UNCLOGGING YOUR PIPES

I often feel like there is a clot between what I know and what I actually do. I can hear the information but making my impulse-driven brain actually take action is another game entirely. It's a trait that put me off changing all sorts of behaviours in the past, from binge-eating and smoking to people-pleasing and doom-scrolling: I just didn't see myself as someone who was capable of quitting.

Every now and then I've overheard a phrase or learned a fact that has unclogged the pipe between who I am and who I want to be; I call them my 'soul thinners' – like blood thinners but for your principles.

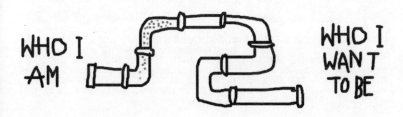

WHO I AM
WHO I WANT TO BE

Kicking the animal-munching habit was the same. While the graphs were good to see, and the numbers interesting, **re-learning about food can often feel like fumbling around for a light switch in the dark,** hoping to find the fact that will illuminate the whole. My hands have found a cheese sandwich on the way to the light switch more than once.

Whatever 'eco conscious' choice you're thinking of making, it's worth looking for these 'soul thinners' – often we're chasing our tails, going over the same questions, when what we really need is a new way of thinking about a topic.

I wanted to share some lesser-discussed ways of thinking about animal products that, for whatever reason, gave me the 'ah hah!' moment that budged a clot inside of me. They're not the usual arguments you hear (THE MEAT INDUSTRY IS EVIL, YOU ARE SELFISH IF YOU EAT ANIMALS, MILK IS POISON!) but they made my half-arse vegan choices *so* much easier.

I HAVE ALREADY MADE THE CHOICE

Shadow was my first pet, a raucous rescue mutt that was an individual in every sense of the word. He had so much personality that he (and by proxy, I) ended up getting expelled from behavioural classes for bad behaviour. Not only did he have personality, he had preferences: the tartan bed over the blue one. He had hobbies: chewing through doors and doing silent, pungent farts that could strip the hair off a badger. He had spirit, he had soul. Even accidentally standing on his paw felt wrong.

Kicking him would have been an appalling act of violence (the UK law agrees, you can get five years in prison for animal cruelty).

The British reverence for pets feels instinctual, irreversible, part of us. We're properly soppy about our cats and our dogs. And when you dig into the facts, it becomes pretty silly to claim that there's any real mental or cognitive difference between most animals categorised as pets, and those creatures filed under 'farm animal'. They too have personalities, preferences, loved ones. They squabble, they learn, they mourn their dead. I realised that what I was trying to do wasn't to decide whether I believed killing animals for pleasure was wrong. I had decided that about thirty years ago. Instead, becoming a half-arsed vegan meant pulling my actions in line with my beliefs. I didn't lack conviction, I lacked moral consistency.

So you see, it's too late for me I'm afraid! Dogs deserve dignity, and so I've got to hang up my hamburgers and go on the hunt for other ways to get my hit of 'hmmmmm! Yum!'

MY TASTES AREN'T INNATE

By the time I went to uni, I had shaken off the idea of romantic predestination. I stopped believing that there was one person out there for everyone in the universe, and instead understood that while *most* people aren't soulmate material, there are probably at least 100 people out of the 7 billion on earth that I would be romantically compatible with. It was up to chance to decide which ones I bumped into, was born near or found myself staring wistfully at through a fish tank.

And yet, until recently, my 'favourite foods' felt like part of me. Who was I? I was Leena! I was a cheese addict! I knew nothing better than my mum's butter shortcake! I had loved pizza longer than I had loved myself.

The idea of giving those up felt like I was contradicting my very nature, forgoing some of my only chances at taste-bud bliss. Halloumi was THE ONE, my Mr Darcy, you can't prise him from my arms!

I had led myself to believe that favourite meals are intrinsic and you can only have so many, but I've started to realise that's as much of a load of old tripe as my belief that Rhys Roberts from the year above me at pre-school was destined to be my husband.

My go-to snacks, or at least the few I'd selected my favourites from, were chosen for me: by the country I was born in, by the income level and preferences of the parents whose home I grew up in, by the choice at the corner shop at the end of my road. If I had been born in rural China, 200 years ago, I can't seriously claim that I'd have been drawing pictures of Freddos in the dust and suggesting we add cheese and baked, sugary beans to the top of our potatoes, can I? A dedication to jacket potatoes is not in my DNA, however much my body makes me feel like it is at 6 p.m. on a Friday.

One example that really surprised me is how little I miss bacon, which is . . . not at all. I still eat tons of delicious savoury snacks and it turns out I just REALLY like salt?!

Kind of embarrassing when you consider all the fuss I made about it. Turns out, the pleasure bacon rashers give can be mimicked by literally anything warm, crispy, fatty and salty. The same goes for my favourite seasoned or processed meats – it was the seasoning I craved, not the meat itself. Coriander, garlic, paprika, caramelised onion, sage . . . that's what I was *really* tasting.

All diets are restricted – by money, time, preference, palette, tradition, availability, medical necessity. By understanding the ways I had been self-restricting, and having a poke around some new supermarket aisles, I'm finding as many vegan favourites as I had meat ones. The best part is, the more of us half-arse it, the more future-favourites will appear on shelves and menus.

I AM NOT A CAVEWOMAN (THANK GOODNESS)

One of my misconceptions about eating meat is that it was fine because 'we' always have.

While it's been debunked that as a species we're hardwired to survive on meat, let's just pretend for a minute that it's true that mankind has always been carnivorous.

It raises two more questions:

1. Do I want the health of my cavewoman great-great-great[100] grandmother?
2. Am I eating the kind of meat they were eating? Is it a fair comparison?

The first one is easy; if I lived in the paleolithic era, my life expectancy would have been thirty-three (so dying . . . right about now) and my most likely cause of death would have been diarrhoea, dehydration or starvation.

So, pass.

Next? Well, as it stands, the World Health Organisation has declared red and processed meat (which made up most of what I ate: beef, pork, lamb, bacon, ham, salami, and any type of sausages I could get my mitts on) *carcinogens*. You know, like the things that cause cancer? The gang includes asbestos, tobacco, alcohol, formaldehyde and ENGINE EXHAUSTS. Of course, they all vary in severity, and carcinogens are things I do OCCASIONALLY consume (asbestos cocktails, but only on my birthday).

However, just like the previous point about pets, I've already decided that, for me, I can't be having carcinogens casually. They CANNOT be an everyday thing; that feels to me like a wild health choice. So, while from a healthy perspective, it's not *wrong* to eat them, it doesn't seem *savvy* to me.

I've got no way of knowing how ancient bison meat compared to a factory-farmed cow today, but it's safe to say it's not quite the same. Either way, I dropped this thought process halfway through because I realised that doing something because we used to do it is a silly way to live; we must do what's best for us, just like our ancestors did. And since we can get all the vitamins, minerals and health benefits we need from plants, and eating meat might be our Great Undoing™, it seems like my great-great-great[100] grannie would probably give my oat milk the thumbs up, all things considered.

In a way, being vegan is a very traditional way to eat, because one of the great human traditions is to adapt what we eat around what will keep us alive.

I AM CHOOSING BETWEEN TWO SELFISH DECISIONS

I think I was a bit worried that if I 'went vegan' I would be holding myself to a moral code I couldn't live up to. That I would scare myself off with my own piety, or scare off others.

It would mean me moving firmly into the camp of 'visibly trying to be a better person' and – unlike clothes shopping or choosing who to bank with – it would have to happen in public. Eating is so frequently a communal activity that there really is no hiding what you're cooking, or ordering, or accepting in the office snack-hand-around. Plus, eating meat and dairy is so publicly prized as a pleasure that outright denying myself that pleasure could come across as pious, an almost saintly sacrifice.

The good news is twofold; since vegan alternatives are genuinely yummy (come and ask me for my god-tier list) and there are plenty of scrumptious vegan foods that everyone eats already (greasy chips, peanut butter, Bisto gravy), I can't claim that I'm really sacrificing pleasure in a big way. Phew for my taste buds *and* my ego.

Secondly, it's kind of selfish to be a vegan. No, really. Read the research (or don't and just trust me, it's pretty grim); if we don't collectively get our meat-munchies under control, we're all in for a rough ride. I'm talking towns under water, limited access to fresh air, no more Internet, Armageddon vibes. It's not cheerful to talk about, but it IS incredibly cheerful to be someone who wants to cling on to lovely luxuries like air, clean water and the Internet. Acting like you want those things is an act of self-honesty and self-preservation. The climate crisis will hit some people worse than others; but it's going to be a party pooper for everyone. Becoming a half-arse vegan is my way of saying 'I quite like the party and I would like to keep dancing.'

There are tons of altruistic reasons to eat a more plant-based diet if you're looking for them. It's just that being a goody two-shoes is not a prerequisite. Selfish bastards welcome.

So, there you have it: some drain cleaner for my moral conundrums. Yours might be different, there are hundreds out there. Next time you meet someone who is vegetarian or vegan, ask them what some of their 'ah ha' moments were. If they sound savvy, steal them.

WHY IT'S BETTER TO BE A BAD BUT CHATTY VEGAN THAN A SECRETLY ANGELIC VEGETARIAN

I had been vegetarian since the beginning of 2020, and I'd just started to comfortably settle into my new identity when I was rudely disrupted by a horrible revelation.

You see, most of the time, I replaced the spaces in my meals that meat had left with dairy or egg products. No meat burgers? No problem, I'll have a halloumi burger. No chicken sandwiches? Fine, grab me an egg mayo one.

Based on my childhood understanding of how a farm works, being vegetarian seemed much kinder than being a meat-eater. After all, I believed, the animals don't *have to* die for me to get my munch on, and in story books the cows gladly give up their milk, the chickens lay eggs *for us*, the bees *share* their honey for our toast. It's wholesome, it's sweet, it's . . . total fiction. Still, arguably, if everyone in the farm industry is nice and treats the animals well, we're not doing anything *wrong*, per se. I might not be being sensible or savvy, but I'm totally in the right, right?

No one is more devastated than me to have to correct themselves, but no, Past Leena, sadly not.

As it turns out, my new vegetarian diet wasn't much more 'sensible' or 'right' than my meat-eating one, by my own definition. Most cheese has a higher carbon footprint than pork or chicken, with roughly four slices of cheese being equal to a whole chicken breast.

I just want to hold space for us cheese-lovers here, and acknowledge how much that fact royally sucks. Let's all take a moment to mourn . . .

Moping over, let's get to business. Realistically, if we plastered that fact over every bus in the country, Big Cheese and the dairy industry would still be open for grating. Red Leicester

sandwiches would still fly off fridge shelves at lunchtime,
thousands of pizzas would still be pushed into thousands of
ovens, cheesy chips would still be passed over counters at 1
a.m., stringy and warm and comforting, dripping with—

Sorry, I'm making myself salivate, where were we?

Right. *Even if* every news programme in the country
broadcast those findings (and they've had plenty of time,
they're not new) and every toilet stall door had a pie chart
of cheesy carbon emission plastered to it, I'm not convinced
much would be different.

So, what *does* change our minds?

People.

But not just any people. *Probably not* the well-informed
vegan activist in a documentary, or the person who posts the
preachy infographic on Instagram. Not the shouting
leafleteers in the town centre or the politicians who tout their
devotion to a 'greener future'. Potentially not even me.

When we hear information from the people who are already
in our lives, and we can also see that they are acting on that
information, we are much more likely to be able to absorb
that information and respond to it ourselves. When I hear
information from a stranger, be that in the street or on my
phone, it becomes overwhelming because I'm not just
processing what they're saying. I also have an internal
monologue running that asks:

Who is this person?
Can I trust them?
Do they have an ulterior motive?
How do I know if this is relevant to me?
Do I have time for this right now? Should I bookmark this and come back to it later/take a leaflet and read it later?
If it's true, what am I supposed to do about it?!

When a long-term friend started telling me a bit about their veganism, I already knew they didn't have stocks in Beyond Meat, Inc. I *knew* they weren't easily radicalised and usually had a very balanced approach to things. I knew that they knew me, and were bringing the subject up at a time when I had space to process it, and would explain it to me in a way I understood. Because they understood me.

It also felt more plausible that they were telling the truth because they were *acting* on it. It wouldn't have mattered to me whether they were following a strict vegan diet or simply cutting out where they could; the bar is low. Simply some signal that they were convinced enough by it to start tweaking their own lives was enough. They were also from a similar socio-economic background to me, and they had similar socialising and work patterns, so when I asked them questions about how they cut down on their dairy, they could give examples that were truly relevant to my life; down to which vegan swaps were currently good at our local supermarket, and which were a rip-off.

What I found so interesting about reading the work of Ed Winters (one of the famed online vegan advocates that formed a big part of me becoming a 'bad vegan') is that he is very open about the fact that he has been unsuccessful at convincing any of his close family members to stop eating meat. As the author of a book literally titled *How to Argue With a Meat Eater*, he's the king of thoughtful responses to objections about veganism and an encyclopaedia of factual retorts to common misconceptions. And yet, he himself admits that he'd rather attend a farmer's convention and debate with them about meat rather than attend a family party where he has to explain his choice of meal.

When I read that, I was reminded of researcher Meg Jay's work on identity capital and weak ties. She discusses it in the context of careers; arguing that most people get their greatest opportunities through 'weak' ties: contacts in their outer circle, not their nearest and dearest. According to her, information 'spreads farther and faster through weak ties than through close friends because weak ties have fewer overlapping contacts'. It tallies with Malcom Gladwell's findings in his much-applauded work *Tipping Point*, in which he discusses the phenomena of social epidemics and how ideas spread throughout a population. One of his findings is that trends, rumours and behaviour changes that happen rapidly are often set into motion by a small number of people who move through overlapping social groups 'spreading' the idea. These people fall into three categories – connector, maven and salesperson – and (usually unwittingly) 'tip' the balance of a society simply by the way they connect with others.

In my own experience, this makes sense. Growing up, I knew a total of one vegetarian, my brother's girlfriend. In my inner circle, I didn't (and still don't) have anyone who is a strict vegan; but as the years passed, and the world started slowly changing, chatty, friendly vegan people have moved into my peripheral circles, and when I became curious, I immediately knew who I could approach to know more. No one ever sat me down and said 'Leena, we need to have a talk about how many sausages you are consuming on a hungover Sunday morning!' They simply existed, openly eating in the same space as me (at conferences, in workplaces, at mutual friends' birthday parties) and being open to questions about veganism, imperfectly equipped as they might have been to answer every question, or defend every meal they ever ate.

It's no surprise that as I've gotten older, more 'weak tie' vegans have appeared in my life. Between 2023 and 2024 it's been estimated that the number of vegans in the UK has risen by 1.1 million, and, if projections are correct, we'll be fifteen million strong by 2025. Comedian David Mitchell, in an article he wrote for the *Guardian* about how he'd noticed the shift, said that the annoying thing about the new surge of vegans 'is the nagging suspicion that they might be right. When there were hardly any vegans, I hardly ever had to think about that.'

It's my guess that the future will not be vegan. Not completely. It is clear though, simply on the basis of logistics, that meat will become much more expensive and much less available. We simply don't have the resources or the land to keep producing it at the rate we are now. It's probable that meat will become much more of a 'treat' food than an everyday occurrence. It's very likely that if you don't become 'the vegan friend', you *will* have significantly more of them.

It occurs to me that perfect sincerity isn't how we win; it will be sheer volume. Of course, I know that the dream of PETA directors is that hordes of civilians overnight flush their cupboards of 'impure' food products and take to the streets with placards. I also know that, among us placid Brits at least, that is never going to happen.

The more half-arse vegans there are out there, with our (hopefully) less intimidating presence, admitting that we slip up constantly but are unwilling to continue denying the facts, the more likely you are to know us. We're in your office, we're in your knitting circle, we're at your gigs. We're your cousin's new boyfriend, we're your dad's mechanic, we work in your local pub. We wrote a book you bought and are now (slightly) regretting reading.

Veganism as a restrictive diet, a ritualistic cleansing or a virtue signal makes the problem of food personal and private. It's a way we fix the dark parts of us that lurk in the corners of our character. The moral track is: *only monsters eat meat*. To stop, you have to at first see yourself as monstrous, and, once you redeem yourself, you must start seeing everyone around you as monstrous too.

To be a 'half-arse' vegan is to turn away from that, so far, largely ineffective line of thinking. It's recognising that it wasn't *you* who created the meat-consuming culture you were born into, you didn't choose how the shelves were stocked in your supermarket or what poor nutritional scare-stories you've been taught as a child. It's accepting that, while eating meat and dairy might have served beautiful functions in your community previously, it is about to become one of the ways we destroy ourselves as a species. It's promising to not ignore the facts, or be a bystander anymore, but slowly back away from the edge in the best way *you* feel safe, as fast as is possible for you.

And it's not being ashamed to bellow 'oi! Cliff!' as someone approaches the edge, despite the fear of someone shouting back 'if cliffs are SO BAD, why are you still anywhere near it?!'

Saying you *are* vegan, whether that's a 'half-arsed vegan' or a 'bad vegan' means we're all agreeing on a direction. It might come with caveats, and 'cheat days' and a very, very slow transition, but we're allowing ourselves to be vocal about the solution and refusing to bear it alone. If the creation of the food system was a group effort, the solution has to be communal too. It isn't the pious vegans, but the chatty ones that are going to tip the balance. The only way we're going to get out of this is to eat our way out, and that won't be a shameful canteen lunch eaten in a toilet cubicle; it'll be a banquet that everyone is invited to.

WAYS TO START BEING A HALF-ARSE VEGAN

Here are ten ways of starting to align your plate with what you reckon is savvy and sensible, without (dun dun duuun) cutting out cheese. Or the occasional Curly Wurly. Or finding yourself ironically driving fifty miles in a gas-guzzling car to track down a chickpea sandwich. You might still get into trouble with yourself regarding the 'right' category, but I really believe that once a choice seems more doable to us, we're much more able to enter into the theoretical debate. Annoyingly, I've found veganism to be a lot like my jogging habit. At the beginning, it took all my energy to get me to the end of my street. Now I find that having a good run gives me more energy for the day, and slowly but surely I've been able to run a little more easily every month. Learning to cook one vegan meal felt like turning my eyelids inside out when I first started, but as the small tasks *became* low energy through practice, I was able to edge towards more challenging switches whilst still only using a half-arse amount of spirit to get me there.

Here are some half-arse vegan suggestions. Pick one and stick with it. Pick one and cheat on it. Pick two and alternate depending on the week. Remix them, trim their ends, prod them until they look doable. Try each one until you find one that doesn't drive you up the wall. Whatever you do, get just a bit of your bum on the seat.

1. Breakfast Vegan

This one is your entry level easy-peasy switch – don't worry about what you eat the rest of the day, but pledge to make every breakfast vegan. Unlike lunches and dinners, breakfasts usually have only a few ingredients and are often eaten alone, making them the least admin-heavy and emotionally charged meal to start experimenting with. Crack out the peanut butter on toast, pile the dairy-free pancakes

high or whack some oat milk and blueberries on your
Weetabix.

2. Brand Vegan

This is a zero-effort rule that simply involves you moving
your hand slightly to the side when you reach for your
supermarket staples. If the brand you usually buy from
makes a vegan alternative, *that* is what goes in your basket.
Every week more household names are testing the waters
with new products: Cathedral City, Richmond, Heinz,
Boursin, Options and even Lindt chocolate. Your pledge
is to be there to boost those sales figures whenever they
release one of these experiments into the market, and make
sure those 'limited editions' become permanent fixtures in
your branch. By buying products that are already in your
cupboard circulation, the differences should be almost
undetectable to your change-resistant brain. Even if
you're not 100 per cent vegan, you'll be doing your local
vegans a solid.

3. Tag Vegan

When we prioritise impact over identity, we can really start
to tag-team and get thinking about this challenge collectively.
Grab a pal who also feels like they can't commit to a vegan
diet full time and Frankenstein together a whole vegan diet
for a month. Make a monster. Half each. You can take a look
at your calendars and pick which days would be best for each
of you, or set general deals like 'I'll do all the breakfasts, and
every other lunch.' If someone slips up, or needs a hall pass,
no worries – you can simply text to switch or make up for it

by going out for a vegan meal together! It's also a great excuse to keep in touch and talk about delicious food all month long. Where there would have been NO vegan diet, you have made ONE vegan diet 'happen', together. Cute.

4. Eat Out Vegan

If, when you're out, there's a vegan option, you *have* to order it and try it. That's it, that's the dare. I love this one because it requires no extra cooking skill on my part: I'm already paying to have someone else cook for me so I might as well make the most of it. It also makes ordering much faster, and you get to try weird and wonderful things you've never wrapped your gob around before. Level up and make it a rule: *when you're out, don't eat the snouts*. Or something. I'll keep workshopping the slogan.

5. Eat In Vegan

You guessed it: when you're IN, it's vegan. This is a better option if you live somewhere where you're more likely to find pickled alien on the menu than a vegan option, or you have other dietary requirements that rarely mesh well with a standard vegan dish in a restaurant. Gluten-free half-arsers, I feel for you. This one means stocking your kitchen with delicious vegan condiments and switching your staple batch-cooks for vegan alternatives and, honestly, it's a lot of fun. It also means you up the novelty of your eating-out experiences, making animal products much more of a 'treat' than a passive necessity – it's like time travel, you're living in the future!

6. Snack Vegan

If switching meals feels daunting to you, or you live in a household where you're not in control of the menu, making your snacks vegan is a great way to go. There's a whole world of flavoured nuts out there, just waiting for you. Raid your local supermarket for their weird and wonderful new imports, get creative with your popcorn for a night in and (yawn, but necessary) it might be a good way to prompt your brain into snacking on fruit and veg in those nibbling-cus-I'm-bored moments. It's also a great excuse to throw a taste-test party to find your new favourite snacks. Get everyone to bring all the weird vegan chocolate and cheese they can carry. It's always touch and go so hilarity will inevitably ensue, just make sure you take reaction pictures. Least flattering wins.

7. Condiment Vegan

Did you know that your favourite condiments almost all have vegan equivalents? Mayo, pesto, stock cubes, gravy . . . in fact, some of the instant gravy brands are already (albeit accidentally) vegan. Condiments are a way I passively ate animal products without even really noticing – or even enjoying. As they're mostly used as an ingredient or topping, and usually get most of their flavour from the other things in them like the, err . . . flavouring. I've found that the vegan swaps have been mostly indistinguishable from the original. I also use condiments in smaller quantities and buy them less often than I do the main parts of my meals, which means that even if I do have to put in a little more effort into hunting them down, it's way less of a faff overall.

8. No Swap Vegan

If you're currently a vegetarian but you usually replace the part of your meal that would have been meat with a dairy/ egg alternative, try replacing it with a genuinely animal-free substitute. As I mentioned earlier, when I first began to give up meat I would opt for halloumi instead of bacon in my fry-up or an omelette instead of a steak when I was out. Cheese bites got bunged into the oven instead of chicken nuggets when I was at home, that sort of thing. Take a look at your go-tos and see if you can switch out the 'missing meat' section of your meal for tofu, chickpeas, faux meat. Or, you could even reimagine the meal altogether so it doesn't revolve around a meat replacement as the 'star'.

9. Nigella Vegan

Nigella is nice, but feel free to switch her out for your favourite chef's first name: Delia, Ainsley, Gordon, Rick, Nadiya . . .

This one is great if you find your brain works 'in meals' rather than according to rules. One of the big ways I started to feel confident that I *might* be able to switch to eating mostly vegan, was easing my way in by learning some simple vegan recipes. It will be an even better option for you if you actually *like* cooking (I have really tried, but alas).

Your challenge is to become your own personal chef for a certain period of time (a week? A month?) and your target is to find your *new favourite* vegan dish. When I did this I found a very delicious peanut butter chilli that is now my go-to batch-cooking Sunday recipe. This challenge gives you a great excuse to experiment, and to circumnavigate new aisles of your supermarket, as well as to make an occasion out of cooking for the people you live with.

Now, when your brain thinks about trying to go vegan but then roars 'but what would I eat?!', you'll have a whole list of answers stuck to your fridge.

If you really aren't a big home-cooker, you can always customise this challenge and make it your goal to find your *new* favourite eat-out meal or restaurant. I will let you cheat like that. It is, of course, in the spirit of half-arsing.

10. Points Mean Prizes Vegan

I don't know about you, but my brain doesn't respond well to a telling off. It does however respond very well to: stickers, stars, badges, little treats. When I did my own 'points mean prizes' version of Veganuary, I knew there were thirty-one days in January, which offered the potential for ninety-three vegan meals. I kept a record of how many of those meals I managed to make vegan by sticking a shiny sticker on my calendar for every vegan meal I ate. Each sticker was a 'point'. I had thresholds for rewards I'd give myself at the end of the month, depending on how many points I scored. At 40 points I'd get a solo trip to the cinema to see any guilty pleasure I liked. At 60 I'd get a day out to a favourite nearby town. In the end (and no one was more surprised than me) I ended up scoring 87 and rewarding myself with a new pair of (bright red, extremely eccentric) glasses that I probably needed anyway for, you know, seeing, but had never permitted myself to buy as a second pair of glasses felt like an unnecessary luxury. The incentives can be tailored to whatever will tempt you to keep going, they don't need to be spending-centric and you can definitely rope in loved ones to help with the rewards (forty-minute back rub, anyone? Hoovering amnesty for a month?).

In the past I'd often worked on the challenge model of 'all or nothing' – and if I slipped up, I would throw in the towel. It might feel childish but a positive reinforcement system based on your *overall* wins rather than focusing on a moment of weakness can get you much further than you might expect. And you can proudly be your true petty, competitive, wonderful, childish self, the one who loves stickers over restrictions.

This is not an exhaustive list. Maybe you could become a caffeinated vegan (all your hot drinks are vegan) or, when you're dishing out dinner, you could start to split the portion of meat you'd usually serve one person across two plates. The ways to be a half-arsed vegan are as varied as the people chowing down. What matters is that you start.

An unexpected side effect of becoming a half-arse vegan for me is the self-confidence it's given me. It sounds silly, but when it comes to making rational, calm and non-fear-based decisions around food, I used to place very little faith in myself. I have always suspected that I'm someone who loves to sit around pontificating about justice, but is too scatty or careless to actually put what I believe in to practice. I was doomed to forever be an armchair activist.

Slowly switching showed me that I can still be spontaneous around food, but that it was okay to start slowly separating all the strands of what made up my 'default' diet. Whilst on the whole there seems to be evidence that the prevalence of eating disorders is lower among vegans, if you've had issues in the past it's true that it's sensible to tread carefully. It's one of the reasons I'm so against purity culture within the vegan movement, because while we'll all need to disembark HMS *Meat Mania* eventually, the way we each jump ship will be very different.

Some people love the rush of a cold plunge off the deck into the freezing water of (pardon the pun) cold turkey. New year's resolutions suit a wild swimmer with an all-or-nothing mentality.

Others will need to sit in the still-attached lifeboat for a little while, looking over the edge, maybe lowering themselves and testing the water first. As long as we can all agree that the ship will eventually sink (and that standing on deck playing the fiddle, pretending it's not happening is a very silly plan – this is not the *Titanic*) I think it's okay to trust people to find their own exit strategy.

At the time of writing, I haven't touched a bit of cheese in over four months. Will I ever again? Probably. I am half-arsed like that. But you better believe I'll be saving myself for the most succulent, decadent slice, on an occasion where I'm celebrating and I will require complete reverent silence so as to enjoy every last morsel.

No more sad cheese sandwiches swallowed whole in a car park. No more passive gulps that don't make much difference to me but make all the difference to the future of the planet. My stage directions no longer read: [exit, pursued by Stilton].

Shame has never been an agent for change, only temporary obedience. Instead of debating whose fault it is that we're in quicksand, we could be clubbing together and clambering out. Whatever the eco-change you're looking to make, whether it's ducking meat where possible, getting the sleeper train over the short-haul flight, or switching where you buy your socks . . . it's important to know your reasons for tweaking your life, in light of the lava. Don't let anyone tell you that an oat milk hot chocolate with real squirty cream is a contradiction – it's a wink in the direction of a better future you can see looking back at you, across the room.

Right, back to work and then not long until we can finally head home . . .

Half-Arse Home

—

'Mummy, I want to go home!'

So screeches every toddler who has Had Enough™ and would like to be beamed back to base. 'Going home' doesn't just mean going home; it's code for 'I need rest'/'I need less stimulation'/'I need to feel safe'/'I have seen enough'/'I need shelter from this cruel world.'

I still now, at thirty-four, often feel the urge to bellow at the sky:

'I WANT TO GO HOME!'

But that isn't always how 'home' functions for us these days. Stressed out about your job, your body, your career, the state of the world? Want to go home? Too bad, because perfectionism will pursue you there too.

Instead of a sanctuary, our homes have become yet another to-do list, a project to sharpen and preen. The piles that clutter it, the bland walls that line it, aren't just impractical or boring, they have become a source of real shame. During a particularly frantic part of my twenties I would quite literally stay out longer after work to avoid returning to my flat which, through stress and negligence, looked like someone had ransacked a wheelie bin, my belongings strewn like sad confetti over every possible surface.

Whilst some people love home renovations and interior design daydreaming, I know I'm not alone in feeling like the standards for how aesthetically pleasing our homes should be are at best a little ambitious, and at worst utterly soul crushing.

There must be a middle ground between running our homes like plush hotels and effectively living in a bin; but to half-arse it, we have to first discover why the bar is so high, and who put it there . . .

THE RECENT ORIGINS OF THE IDEAL HOME

Although the royal and regency cinematic universes would have you thinking otherwise, for the majority of human history, for the majority of people, home, if they had one, was not a stage for public displays of their excellent taste in interiors. It was considered adequate if it had the basics. If you wanted a bigger house, it was because you were planning on filling it with people, not objects.

Flash forward to today, and our homes aren't just a place to eat, wash and rest; they are the backdrops to our lives. Whether we're simply taking Zoom calls from our kitchen table, FaceTiming our far-flung family or broadcasting a DIY bathroom makeover to friends and strangers on social media, our homes have become much more visible, even if you're not working in the public eye. I'm admittedly participating in it; as someone who works at home as a full-time online creator, hundreds of thousands of people have seen the headboard of my bed, the view from my dining table, the kettle I boil every day and the mangy towel that hangs on my bathroom door. It's not only my grotty abode that's on show; we are all bombarded by content showcasing the homes of the rich and famous. This was true even before social media came on the scene. It began (arguably) with the televised tours of the White House started by Jackie Kennedy in the 1960s, before moving on to programmes like the hit nineties show *MTV Cribs*. More recently there has been the online phenomena of house tours made by *Architectural Digest*, in which informally delivered personal home tours from the likes of Jennifer Aniston, Naomi Campbell and Travis Barker have garnered hundreds of millions of views.

It might have been male writers who authored my unrealistic expectations for love (thanks for nothing, Nicholas Sparks), but it was female directors who set my younger self's gold standard for 'home'. It was in the unfussy warm corners of cosy rooms, created by Nora Ephron and Nancy Meyers, that I pictured I would someday curl up with a book, in my Adult House, occasionally wandering off for a snack break in my Adult Kitchen, before draping myself over my Adult Kitchen Island to drink wine. You almost certainly have the blueprint for one of these homes sitting in your subconscious: *The Holiday*, *When Harry Met Sally*, *The Parent Trap*, *You've Got Mail*, *It's Complicated* . . . They were characterised by their light and cushy elegance, lived-in but stylish, the architectural equivalent of a cup of cocoa blended with a cashmere jumper.

And then there are the celebrity homes with their crystal bath tubs, their glass-blown chandeliers, gold-leaf wallpaper and perfectly polished reclaimed wood floors. From a guest house dedicated only to storing trainers to indoor bowling alleys and underground pools, they immerse us in a world where phrases like '*master* bathroom' and 'indoor swing set' are commonplace, where people build fireplaces *especially* to hang Christmas stockings, and have cupboards dedicated to storing their candle collection and novelty ice machines in every room.

The trickle-down effects of the pressures to endlessly customise and personalise our homes show up clearly in the numbers: the interiors market has seen a boom in the last ten years: globally valued at $121 billion in 2016 and projected to reach $200 billion by 2025. This might be all right if it was churning out stuff we really liked and would cherish for ever; but it looks like the opposite is happening. In my country alone we're chucking out almost 70 million bits of homeware each year; that's around £2.2 billion worth of homeware items being sent to landfill annually. Clearly, we are not as impressed as we should be, given how much we're collectively shelling out.

Is it any wonder that we have a consumer weakness in our need to feel at home? In the UK, the number of people who are renting rather than owning their home has jumped up by a quarter since 2010. If you're aged between eighteen and thirty-four and live in the UK, you're statistically more likely to be living with your parents (40 per cent) than living in your own home with children (20 per cent). When we look at the ratio of house prices to earnings, homes have not been this pricey since 1876. EIGHTEEN SEVENTY-SIX. Queen Victoria was on the throne. The car was yet to be invented. Charles Dickens had only been dead six years.

Through my twenties and into the beginning of my thirties, my landlords (of whom there were nine) made sure I remembered that I was merely camping in their homes. No pets, no parties, no painting, no removing their ugly furniture, no hanging pictures, no replacing the curtains . . . I recently read an article about a few landlords in London who have tried to ban their tenants from having sex, or even having people stay over. We're a generation (or two) who are perpetually sleeping under the parental eye, be it our own or someone else's. It's projected of my generation, the Millennials, that one third of us will never own our own home and, of those who will, half will be renting until their forties.

So, is it any wonder that when a salesman in a big coat saunters in and shows us all the accessories we can buy to make us *feel* like we have a personalised, safe and permanent place to stay, we fill our boots? That rug that transforms the room, the vase that gives the living room that perfect sense of grace, those cushions that punch some much-needed life into that sagging sofa. These aren't bad things to enjoy, if you're truly benefiting from them. But we shouldn't feel inadequate if we haven't mastered the art of interior cohesion. We have to remember that domestic beauty isn't the high standard we should hold ourselves to; it's the opposite really. It's a poor substitute, a low bar that sits below what we really deserve: a true home. All the icing in the world does not manifest the cake beneath it.

Once I realised that my never feeling *quite* 'at home' as an adult had very little to do with the layout of my furniture, or my failures in picking the perfect bedspread or organising my stuff in a perfect KonMari Method – and much more to do with the fact that, on some level, I could not ignore the fact that I was living in someone else's property, my sense of home-shame started to shift. And, as I dug deeper into the aspirational interiors I had held up against my own ramshackle hideout, I started to notice some cracks. Those high aspirations of 'home', the standards that we're often berating ourselves for not meeting, might be more of a mirage than it first seems.

In an interview for *Vulture* magazine, filmmaker Nancy Meyers (who gave us *The Holiday*, *The Parent Trap*, *It's Complicated* and more) laments the 'architecture porn'-focused critics that talk so much about the interiors of her movies and perhaps miss what is at the heart of them. For her, what is important isn't the aesthetics of the houses her characters inhabit. These are merely functional, a way to breathe life into people we only get to spend a short ninety minutes onscreen with. It's a fast way to familiarise us with her characters. It is a shorthand for what we wish we had: more time with them.

It's this aspect of time that comes up again for the co-author of my interior fantasies, Nora Ephron (*When Harry Met Sally*, *You've Got Mail*, *Julie & Julia*). In her essay for the *New Yorker*, 'Moving On: A Love Story', she reflects on her delusional love affair with an increasingly expensive apartment that she had felt was a part of her. She describes the scales falling from her eyes as the rent increased: this place was never hers; she was only borrowing it. She starts to disentangle herself from the aesthetics of 'home', accepts that the relationship was one-sided, that the building did not love her back, and begins a more pragmatic affair with a smaller, more affordable abode in a cheaper part of town. She ends her description of all the things she loves about her new rental with a comfortable realisation: 'it's not home. It's just where I live.'

Perhaps, if the authors of our interior fantasies have stopped giving a shit, it's all the permission we need to follow suit. In focusing on the aesthetics of our homes, we risk missing the characters that move through them. Unlike the characters in our most beloved movies, we have the luxury of getting to spend *more than ninety minutes* with the people and the places we love. Much like with personal style, perhaps we are in danger of using meticulous colour palettes as a shorthand for forming a relationship with our space; perhaps, the more possible it is to *buy* that feeling of home, the less we will focus on what makes it actually so. Namely: autonomy, ownership, longevity. All things that can't be fully given in a rent or mortgage market, with imperfect local democracy and some serious sewage issues. What makes a home isn't a perfect aesthetic, it's the permission to stay and be safe there, however dishevelled. I loved a detail I learned about the home created for Meryl Streep's character in Nancy Meyers' *It's Complicated*. Apparently, Meryl arrived on set and immediately declared it was much too nice, and suggested Meyer add some water damage to dishevel the home a little. Obviously, she was obeyed: who argues with a woman who has the ability to become Miranda Priestly at any moment?!

When it comes to the 'real' homes of celebrities, there seems to be an element of fiction to them too, at least in the long term. Kendra Gaylord dug into the data behind the famed *Architectural Digest* tour videos and discovered that 29 per cent of celebrity houses featured on the show have been sold since the videos about them went live, mostly within two years. Many sell *because* of their appearance on the channel, for astronomically more than their normal market value. Some even sell before the videos go live. The 'house flip' nature of these projects, transforming property for profit with aesthetic upgrades or by association alone, means that celebrities can reappear on the series every few years with a new 'for ever home' to flog for profit. It's absolutely fascinating to see how someone might design a home when money is no object (although I find it hard to begrudge Cara Delevingne her 'vagina tunnel': a burrow dressed in pink fluffy flaps that leads from her fireplace, through a wall, before ending as a faux washing machine in her kitchen?); but it's clear that the creators of these interior worlds we fantasise about aren't as infatuated with them as we are.

What we want to be intimate peeks into the lives of people we admire, and so desperately want to feel like we know, are actually property listings with a soundtrack. Unlike those aspirational houses we spend so much time (however involuntarily) looking at, our own homes are not plot devices, photoshoot backdrops or commodities for profit. They're real places, where we live our *real* lives. And in our real lives there is no set designer matching the curtains with our character quirks, no team of cleaners or stylists to lavish aesthetic bliss on our lives. It's just us; running through rooms trying to keep both earrings in our ears and our keys from being eaten by the back of the sofa. How, in the grand myriad of life's flurries, are we supposed to maintain a home that looks like a Nora Ephron character could waltz into it at any moment?

The good news is, we're not meant to.

There's that old adage from the artist and writer William Morris: 'Have nothing in your house that you do not know to be useful, or believe to be beautiful.' What reads to some as a justification to declutter our homes of 'ugly' and wanton decor and go on an Anthropologie binge was, originally, anything but. Morris was a (flawed) activist with a penchant for socialism who was fervently against the kind of industrial manufacturing that birthed interior-decorating mainstays like IKEA. In fact, he would have both grinned and grimaced at what researchers call 'The IKEA Effect'.

The IKEA Effect describes the phenomenon of humans valuing something more highly, or becoming more attached to an item, if we have a hand in its production; regardless of its objective quality. There are even research papers on it with titles like 'Bolstering and Restoring Feelings of Competence via The Ikea Effect'. For some reason, the human brain becomes more attached to an item if we have been the one to assemble it, even in its most diluted form or at the end of a process. Whether we're 'building' a Subway sandwich or customising a Starbucks drink, coaxing wonky screws into the base of a sagging IKEA desk or shoving a plastic heart into the depths of a soft toy and then stitching it up, the exploitation of the IKEA Effect can be seen all over customer-facing industries. My favourite example is that of Betty Crocker, who cashed in after a failed launch of their 'easy' instant cake mix (*just add water!*). They found that by changing the recipe so that you also had to add an egg, making the process *harder* for the customer, the cake mixture sales soared. Adding an egg made us feel like we were truly participating in the process, practically *real bakers*, and we ate it up, literally. The Decision Lab describes these kinds of business models as 'centred on having us pay for our own labour. We may overlook the fact that we're getting a bad deal to have the satisfaction of assembling it.'

While in commercial circles it's a clever trick, I can't help but think that below all that sleight of hand is evidence for a universal, very sweet (and potentially planet-saving) instinct.

Look at anyone who is retired, well and unburdened by the restraints of employment and you can see . . . WE WANT TO MAKE STUFF. Crochet blankets, whittled birds, garden sheds, allotments – they can't help themselves. We can laugh, but it is also fascinating to observe what people do when they don't *have* to do anything. My hope doesn't come from the beautiful houses I have pinned on Pinterest, but the knowledge that, even though we often give in to the impulse to get something quick, pristine and cheaply made, the science shows that deep down, we'd rather have our grubby, incomplete, homemade thing. Given the time and resources, we return to manual craft as our default.

So, what does that mean for our yearning for a perfectly formed home? That we should take up woodwork and learn to whittle our own chairs? Stage a heist in order to steal enough capital to be able to buy a two-bedroom house, outright?

Sounds like a lot of work to me, and, after all, aren't we here to half-arse it? There has to be a stoop to sit on between outright home-owning and becoming a carpenter, so let's look for it . . .

YOUR HOME IS ALREADY A MIRACLE

My grandfather was a lively but odd man, by all accounts. He died before I'd mastered the art of sitting up but during his life he bounced around a plethora of odd jobs: he was a painter decorator, he opened a shop called Normington's (for which I still have some branded brown paper bags), he ran a foster home, and he was also a self-taught plumber. He had little education, little expendable income, and he didn't leave us any great stores of money or property. Yet what remained of him after he died were two heirlooms that graced our house as I was growing up: a full, pristine set of royal blue *Encyclopaedia Britannicas* and a handmade wooden bookshelf to store them on.

The family lore goes that he saved and scrimped all of his money and slowly bought up each volume one by one: a book for each letter of the alphabet. It was a collection that took him decades to complete, but this, more than any other comforts he could have furnished his family's home with, was the priority. This might seem absurd to some, but I can see where he was coming from. It was the fifties, he was a working-class war veteran with an unactualised love for words who hoped for more for his children: why *wouldn't* a whole set of encyclopaedias seem like a great bet?

All of the knowledge of the world? Wrapped up and safe in your house? No subscription fee? No need to enter a certain club or attend a certain university? No need to beg for access or permission? To be able to find the answer to your most obscure trivia question on a whim, even if the itch of curiosity struck you in the middle of the night? (Oh, Grandad, you would have loved Wikipedia.) A fortress of facts that would sustain the generations of Normingtons that came after him? The purchase that would ensure his descendants could never be shut out of the world of information again? I'm sure it felt like a *bargain*.

When the time came for me to start studying, these books were no longer the most accurate or most efficient way for me to access any kind of data about the world. Although perhaps not as useful as he may have hoped, his investment was, however, far from obsolete. Their presence, on his handcrafted bookshelf, sitting in the back of our kitchen as we mulled around them speaking of phenomena he could only have dreamed of, made a big impression on me, even though I didn't realise it at the time. There is, of course, the central belief that education is worth investing in, that curiosity should be a financial priority. But there's also what their obsolescence represented: a reminder that my life would have blown my grandad's mind.

The way an evening in my house would look to my ancestors is the stuff of dreams: falling down a Wikipedia hole about the Cabinet Office's cat whilst doing three loads of laundry in a row; eating a delicious doughnut I was able to buy at ten o'clock at night, made from ingredients grown all over the world; going to the loo in a toilet that I don't have to share with my neighbours; having sex without the moral or legal obligation to raise a child, followed by a warm shower. These are all things that people in my family, born less than a century before me, might have yelped with joy to do.

The fact that my home has clean running water, a range of options for places to sit, a thermostat and a singing doorbell is, in the grand scheme of things, a generational miracle. And, even now, it's still an anomaly compared to a lot of the homes around the world. My house would look like a Star Trek spaceship to my ancestors, despite the fact that social media would have me believe it's a stylistic failure.

Thinking of him, of Ron, of all the family homes that have come before my own, I start to make a list of all the things that to me, at the bare bones of it, make a house or apartment into a home:

- A place I can retreat to and find unconditional safety
- A place I can be honest in, no filter required
- A place that meets all my basic needs: warmth, light, a place to wash my body and feed my brain and eat delicious things in peace
- A place where I host the people I love, and gather with others without having to spend a penny
- A place I can stay for as long as I need to, at a price I'll realistically be able to afford for the foreseeable future

It is chilling to me that, for all the Pinterest frame wall inspo and scented candles, amid all of the luxurious corners of my country, this stark list is so hard to tick off for so many people. Even when I was a middle-class renter in a capital city, things like working boilers and natural light were not a given. The incompetence of various landlords meant I often felt like my safety and privacy was intruded on (ever been walked in on while you were eating Weetabix in your pants by an estate agent and couple who want to rent the flat you still have a six-month lease on?).

The bar seems simultaneously extremely high and extremely low among my generation: on the one hand we want our living room to perfectly reflect the textures of our soul; on the other we've become desensitised to paying half of our wages to a landlord who doesn't think that having fully wired lighting is a customer must.

I wish we could fix the housing market and change the fates of everyone up against those wide-ranging experiences that fall under the banner of 'housing insecurity'. That is a huge mission and one that not everyone is called to embark on (although it might be you – stick around for the last chapter on what to whole-arse!). What is important is that we stop seeing our yearning for new candles and home decor as a personal weakness, or a sign of our own superficiality, and recognise what that yearning truly represents: a real need to feel a sense of home, in a world where security is hard to come by.

One of my occasional hobbies is lurking in obscure Facebook groups, and one of my favourites to browse is called 'The Dull Women's Club'. The posts are, as promised, and by most definitions, dull as sin. They marvel at the patterns they can make with their vacuum lines during their carpet cleans; they debate which order they like to put their cutlery away in their cutlery draws; they lovingly track the movement of small spiders through their house; they document the way light refracts through their patio doors. They show off their novelty spatulas, their thrifted teapots, their ripening bananas. And yet the group feels like a collective out breath, almost beautiful in its subversiveness.

What is so wrong with being dull, at least in your own home? To be 'dull' is to be less intense, right? Isn't another word for that '*rest*'? A lack of expectation, or performance, of effort? Isn't it a rejection of the pursuit of a possible 'spectacular' in exchange for a certain 'enough'? Have I scrolled too close to the sun, have I lost the plot? If I have, I'm certainly not alone. 'The Dull Women's Club' is one million members strong. It would seem like the intentional and surprisingly empowering practice of being dull is catching on, and I, for one, am happy to join in. At least half the time.

YOU DO NOT HAVE TO BE A PLANT MUM

As someone who spent the first year of the 2020 pandemic on the top floor of a block of flats with no balcony and windows that only opened to the width of my wrist, I understand the urge to bring the outside indoors. Like many people, the legal restrictions on our access to green spaces made me realise how much I'd taken 'the great outdoors' for granted. Without the power to welch on my rental contact, change the law or devise a vaccine myself in my kitchen, I turned to houseplants. And I wasn't the only one.

A 2019 survey by the Royal Horticultural Society found that nearly three quarters (72 per cent) of adults owned a houseplant – a figure that rose to 80 per cent amongst 16–24-year-olds. Then came the 'botanic boom' of lockdown, when people's collective sense of being deprived of time outdoors was coupled with the rise of houseplant-focused influencers (plantfluencers, if you will) and professional 'Plant Mums', who could, in 60 seconds or less, show you all the weird and wonderful (and pricey) houseplants your home had been missing. British online retailer Patch reported a 500 per cent increase in sales during the first UK lockdown alone.

I started 2020 with one small Chinese money plant, grown from a cutting gifted to me by my friend Sanne. By the time my circulation in the world began to return to 'normal', in 2023, I owned twenty-two.

The downside was . . . I wasn't very good at caring for the indoor botanical jungle I had purchased. If I am a 'plant mum', then I'm the kind of maternal figure that leaves her child at the supermarket, with all the zest for parenting of Miss Trunchbull.

The guilt that comes with looking at the carcass of a plant you have killed feels like a very ancient kind of guilt. The kind that probably has a very practical evolutionary purpose. The kind that, in a wider context, has been dulled through a disconnection to the natural world our body so craves.

My internal monologue chips in:

God, if I can't keep a plant alive, what am I doing with all these other responsibilities in my life?
It's such a simple task, why can't I do it?!
I really should buy another and get it right this time, it would be good for me.

Plants are good for us, aren't they? They clean the air, or something? They're good for our brain chemistry, right? *Right?*

As it turns out, the studies on the benefits of houseplants seem a bit ropey. They are mainly self-reported or subjective ('I feel healthier/happier'), they're done on very small groups of people or applied outside of their area of relevance. A common one is studies of patients in hospitals. It's obvious that a patient who is mentally at a particularly low point without the option to go outside might feel happier with a plant in the room, but that doesn't necessarily mean we should apply these findings to our own mood as we voluntarily sit inside our houses on an average Sunday. Studies that *do* reference any significant biological change are, on closer inspection, actually citing the activity of *repotting* plants (direct contact with soil is known to have measurable benefits), not simply buying them and putting them on our bookshelves. The received wisdom that they improve the air quality in homes has also been widely debunked. Even *National Geographic* admits that, to see any meaningful change in air quality in a small 500 square foot apartment, you would require what would equate to an indoor forest.

While they can't do much good, they can also do an impressive amount of harm. We've seen a lot of coverage of 'fast fashion' in recent years, but the 'fast plant' industry has a pretty high chuck-rate too. We might think of houseplants simply as naturally-occurring plants that have been displaced, but we have to remember that they're the result of mass-production – think of them as closer to agricultural products rather than something that comes from a natural environment, like a rainforest or a wild field.

As with clothes, we often forget that our houseplants will all have had a long, complex history before they ever come into our possession. The journey to our windowsill isn't an easy one. Growing houseplants in huge industrial quantities instead of in a home you're already heating is, as you can guess when you actually think about it, incredibly energy intensive. It takes about a year and a half of heat-controlled, energy-intensive farming to grow a succulent that is ready to sell, anywhere between fifteen months to twelve years to grow a cheese plant (depending on their size) and *fifteen years* for a bonsai tree. They're usually planted in soil that often contains peat, mined from peat bogs, the use of which is, it turns out, a huge carbon emitter. I'd never considered bogs on my list of things to worry about, but some scientists say that they are up there with rainforests as the most important and fragile carbon sinks that keep our ecosystem on the straight and narrow.

And that's just growing them. Once they're mature enough to sell, they can rack up some serious 'plant miles'. As you can imagine, unlike rectangular, stackable, dead objects like books, transporting living, squishable organisms with a list of diva-like demands isn't a terribly energy-efficient process. Most indoor plants for sale in the UK are grown in the Netherlands, Italy and Germany and transported here over long distances in temperature-controlled lorries surrounded by single-use protective material.

When they die (which, more often than not, they do within the year), only 10 per cent of local councils in Britain accept and recycle plastic plant pots, which results in my country popping half a billion of them into landfill every year. EVERY YEAR.

This isn't to suggest that if you are the proud owner of an indoor botanical garden and you've successfully managed to not kill them, you should hang your head in shame. I can see the real symbolic pleasure plants can bring to people's daily routines: injecting delight into the homes of those who are housebound temporarily or permanently, marking the passing of hard days and glum winters. They can be a simple and, in small doses, harmless joy.

I mention the weird industry behind houseplant production only to release those of us whose failure as plant parents weighs heavy on our hearts, and to rid you of the urge to buy more if they don't genuinely add to your life. It's more to try to reject this major tenet of our culture that makes keeping plants alive (in environments that they weren't designed to thrive in, often far from the continents they evolved to survive in) a signifier of whether *we* are capable adults.

I realised that, far from my plants dying being an indication of my inadequacy as a human, the state of my plants spoke volumes about the kind of environment I was expecting *myself* to grow in. Often the flats I was able to rent in the pokey suburbs of London were cramped, dark and left little space for me or my plants to stretch their stems out. The time it had taken for me to commute to, and then work at, the job that paid for said pokey flats left little time for the spacious rhythms of life and the mental wellbeing it took to keep up a routine, a routine that involved say . . . remembering to water plants! As the lockdowns wore on I asked myself what I was doing in a place that barely gave me access to the very basics of life that plants demand: light, air, soil, space. I wondered: if *they* could demand it, maybe I could do the same?

Of course, the easy answer was: move!

Which is something I did in the end; I gave up my office job in central London to go and freelance back near my hometown, where basic amenities are still daylight robbery, but much more manageable for a Millennial-sized wallet.

But that *isn't* the easy answer, is it? Because it's much more complicated than that. It wasn't, and isn't, the answer to all our woes. It can't be, logistically for so many people, and morally for all of us. The answer to a lack of basic needs being met shouldn't be to 'get lucky' (or be privileged, if they are not simply different words to describe different sides to the same phenomenon). It also can't be to simply fill our home with houseplants and 'practise gratitude' for a glimpse of green.

The answer can't be 'bring about the revolution'. I *would* like that, let's definitely keep hacking away at that group project (more of that at the end of the book!) BUT until then, what do you do? If you don't have the flexibility or freedom to move somewhere where the cost-of-living crisis doesn't pack the same punch, how can you give yourself a real dose of space, greenery and belonging without forking out for houseplants you will probably neglect?

For me, the question became not about whether house plants were worth being arsed with, but more why we lean so heavily on them for a feeling of calm, achievement and connection to the natural world. What I wanted to know was *why* that gap was appearing and whether it could be plugged with something better . . .

EXTEND YOUR HOME FOR FREE

While I wasn't able to find much hard evidence beyond houseplants' placebo effect on our minds, I was able to find plenty about how a view of nature improves our 'executive control' (an umbrella term for all the cool things brains do: working memory, our RAM, holding attention, selecting which thoughts to linger on and which to keep out).

Researchers at Yale have confirmed that if you'd like to biologically lower your anxiety, blood pressure and stress hormone levels, or increase your immune system functionality – simply stepping outside into nature is a good bet.

Want to significantly lower the cytokine levels in your blood (sounds boring I know, but too high and it can lead to inflammation and ultimately, autoimmune diseases)? Houseplants won't help you but spending two hours in a forest *will*. Our own microbacteria are healthier when we are exposed regularly to diverse microbes – i.e. being outside. We breathe them in and they are absorbed into our teeth, oral cavities and pharynx – and have a positive effect on our immune system, gut-brain axis and our mental health. IT HAS BEEN PROVEN! Mess about in the soil, and the effects are even stronger. It's been found that the type of bacteria found in mud can stimulate the brain to create serotonin, the chemical we're trying to boost when we take antidepressants.

The evidence mounts the more you dig. Kids who were Scouts or Guides as children tracked to have better mental health in later life, and studies show that spending time in natural environments reduces symptoms of ADHD in children.

And here's the interesting part: even if we can't 'get out there', *just knowing* that the great outdoors is 'out there' helps. Research conducted by Professor Frances E. Kuo looked at the experiences of residents in high-rise apartment buildings, comparing those whose windows looked out on trees and grass, and those that looked out at more barren spaces like vacant lots. When controlling for other factors, it was clear that those who could see even a little bit of greenery and nature outside their windows showed a much better level of executive control, particularly when it came to handling altercations within the household. The same was found of concentration levels for university students with green views from their bedrooms; better all around.

It would seem that whilst introducing farmed placeholders for the natural world in little pots scattered throughout our house does little, simply having the feeling of being surrounded by nature 'out there' has a much more profound effect – and it gets more effective once you get out there yourself.

So, why aren't we?

At the moment, us Brits spend about 1–5 per cent of our lives outdoors, averaging about thirty-two minutes a day – which doesn't sound like a lot, but becomes even more chilling when you learn that the required UN guidelines for prisoners is ONE HOUR of time in the open air every day. AT LEAST.

Prisoners. People who are held CAPTIVE. They're getting more time outside than 74 per cent of toddlers. I have to worry about how much time I've spent fretting over paint colours and the arrangement of my furniture whilst neglecting to give myself the decency of more freedom than a *literal prisoner*. Someone who is in the custody of the state. If there ever was a bigger inspiration to half-arse my house aspirations and get my arse outside, it's that statistic.

Perhaps we can, with half our tongue in our cheek, blame the distractions of the home-improvement industrial complex; but we also have to lay some blame at the feet of urban planning. It's projected that two thirds of humanity will live in cities by the year 2050 (up from the 56 per cent who live in them today), and with little access to nature and dwindling leisure hours, the odds are stacked against any inclination we might have to spend more time outdoors. In my country, England, the public only have access, or what is called 'the right to roam', to 8 per cent of the land. A legacy of private property, a widening wealth gap and a poor public transport network means that spending more time outside becomes not only a radical act, but very logistically tricky.

In city environments, spending time outside, in public, without spending money is a feat in itself. Search the term 'hostile architecture' and you'll realise that our urban planners want us to sit our arses inside. From removing benches to studs on flat surfaces, to failing to provide shade in open spaces or enough public toilets, the powers that be would really rather you either be shopping, or at home fretting about whether your gallery wall is even, or if getting a new kettle will make you like your life more.

You can, however, join the fight for expanding 'home'. From guerilla gardening, where residents of urban areas are taking it upon themselves to rewild and intuitively garden the discarded pockets of green in their neighbourhood, to the campaigns to regain the right to roam our countryside, you'll see little rebellions bubbling up between the paving slabs, if you stop to look closely. As we take a moment to step back from what we're told to put huge amounts of effort into – the personalised design of our small plot of borrowed property – we can see that we're missing out on a much more permanent sense of home, a home that doesn't charge us for entry or threaten eviction for a dusty light switch.

What I find most interesting about watching celebrity house tours is their instinct to reconstruct 'public' spaces within the luxury of their private property. It's not uncommon to see swimming pools with rows of empty deckchairs, underground bars complete with beer taps, skate parks, cinema screening rooms, bowling alleys, dancefloors, and dressing rooms and huge gardens with more benches than their whole family have arse cheeks to fill. Barbra Streisand even built a miniature high street under her house, complete with store fronts and fully fitted retail spaces: she has a sweet shop, a gift shop and even a shop just for dolls. Just like us, they crave public 'third' spaces, neither home nor work. With an unlimited budget, the rich aren't creating a new kind of space, with new purposes; they're recreating what most of us already have access to, for the much cheaper price of having to share it with other people.

When home ceases to be one building, or one street, but becomes a community, a place, a sense of belonging based on more than just bricks and mortar, it's harder to be whipped up into a state of worry about the colour of your curtains. The broader our sense of home becomes, the harder it is to be evicted from it. Our desire to improve on our homes ourselves and fill them with plants might be the misplaced echo of a deeper instinct; to slow down, create what we need with our own hands and get our arses outside. That's bad news for furniture shops and plant centres everywhere, but good news for those of us who have been trying to claw back our time and have spent far too many hours feeling inadequate at the state of our homes. There's simply no need to be so arsed.

One of my favourite poems is Roger Robinson's 'A Portable Paradise'. In it he tells us that his grandmother advised him to keep his 'paradise', his home, hidden on his person. Then, she says, whether you're in a hovel or a hotel, you can empty out your paradise from your pocket and let it fill you with hope until you sleep. I love this image of not giving power to one place to be paradise, but rather it being something personal that no one can take from you.

So, how do we half-arse ourselves home?

MAKE YOUR HOME A HALF-ARSE HAVEN

DEFINE HOME FOR YOURSELF

Make a list of what home really is to you, and stick it on your fridge. If you're ever in a flap about the cleanliness, polish or colour coordination of your home, revisit your list and ask yourself if all of your original qualifiers are still true. If yes, you still have an ideal home by your own standards and you can leave yourself alone, and if not, you have a framework within which to start making changes.

Here's something to start with . . .

ARE YOU AT HOME?
A CHECKLIST

☐ Do you have the keys to the place?

☐ Is there anything in here that is going to kill you in the next 24 hours?

☐ Can you see at least three things that remind you of something nice, or make you feel hopeful?

☐ Does your favourite person still live here? [insert buddy, partner, pet or yourself!]

Then congratulations, you are home!

If you need to hammer the point home to yourself (literally), surround the list with fun pictures of you and the people you love having fun in the house – as messy and as cheap as you like, just get them up there, claim your space and see at a glance all the ways you're making memories in it.

SCHEDULE A JAILBREAK

I have a note stuck to the mirror above my desk that simply says: 'YOU ARE NOT A PRISONER.' It's a silly but simple reminder that getting more time outdoors than someone who is a custodian of the state *should not* be a luxury. It's the boost I need to steal some time and do a small circuit of my neighbourhood, even if it's just for twenty minutes. While a whole hour would be fab, research shows that 120 minutes a week is the minimum you need to nab the health benefits attached to this outdoors malarky, or if you like, seventeen minutes a day.

Plan to be an outdoor cat, at least sometimes. Schedule it in, fight for it, insist on the bare minimum. TAKE THAT LUNCH BREAK IN FULL (remember your training on wage theft). If a friend asks to meet, make it a walk. If you want to catch up with your partner or housemate after work, suggest a turn about the streets. Take that call on a balcony, or in your garden, or whilst roaming your local park.

If you need reminding of the urgency of getting this time in the fresh air, flick back to the list of health benefits of outdoor roaming just a few pages ago. Also, calling it a prison break or a jailbreak makes it feel WAY more like a cinematic adventure and less like a chore to tick off your boring body-admin to-do list. Screen breaks are out, jailbreaks are in.

ASSEMBLE YOUR KINGDOM-ON-WHEELS KIT

If you're renting, or likely to move around a lot, assemble an army of objects that feel like home to you, and can be flattened and packed into small car boots at short notice. My 'portable paradise' kit included a small rug, a framed poster of Amanda Palmer, a foldable reading lamp, a blanket big enough to cover any sofa, a string of flowery lights, and a small ornamental elephant. They can symbolise something important to you or just have become familiar over time. Instead of telling myself 'this room won't truly be *mine* until it's the perfect paint shade', I know that home is where I curl up to read under *that* lamp. It's your micro-kingdom, your durable domain, and you can wheel it around with you no matter what comes your way.

LEAVE YOUR LAIR ALONE

Resist the 'makeover for makeover's sake' mindset. Next time you get the urge for an impulsive over-turn of your space, ask yourself what kind of hit you're craving? Usually mine can be appeased with a creative session in a sketchbook, a good knitting session or, if I really want to feel the refreshment buzz, I pick up an inexpensive second-hand item that will pack a punch. For me, a big throw or a garish charity shop ornament for the centre of a table does the trick. A before and after moment is great, but a slowly accumulated home is more affordable and much more sustainable. Just like a good painter constantly sketches and revisits and adds to their work as they go, and doesn't just chuck all the paint at a canvas in one day (mostly) – your home will be more thoroughly and long-lastingly 'you' if you allow yourself to tweak and layer the choices over months or even years.

HOMEWEAR HUNTER'S GUIDE

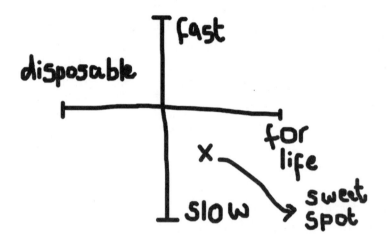

BE YOUR OWN IKEA

Activate the IKEA effect for good by consuming more slowly and trying to make what you need. I've managed to make everything from bathmats to cushion covers to draft excluders, tea towels and curtains for our house – and if anyone suggests getting rid of them any time soon, they can do so over my cold dead body! You can also activate the IKEA effect by restoring and fixing what you already have; making your wonky, imperfect mark! Inserting yourself into the process of creating something is a surefire way to make sure you don't treat it as disposable. It takes time, but once it exists, it's in my house for ever.

HORIZONS OVER HOUSEPLANTS

In place of houseplants, start planting a chance for you to
glimpse the outside world. If you have windows that look
out on greenery, rearrange your furniture so that those trees
or shrubs catch your eye as often as possible. You could even
think about the frequency with which you use each room,
and switch their functions according to where you spend the
most time. Of course, we can't always control the kind of
housing we can access, but that doesn't mean we can't
benefit from this phenomenon. No window? No worries!
The researcher S. Kaplan found evidence to suggest that
simply looking at pictures of beautiful landscapes can have
a positive effect on our cognitive abilities. Just ten minutes
(ten minutes!) looking at Nova Scotian scenery upped
participants' concentration abilities considerably compared to
when they looked at pictures of cityscapes under identical
circumstances. So, in lieu of scenic views, stick some
landscape pictures on your walls, particularly in spots where
you're likely to gaze absentmindedly, like above desks, near
where you wash up, or where you might fold laundry.

BECOME A BREEDER NOT A COLLECTOR

If you insist on having houseplants but don't have a great
track record with keeping them alive (I still have a few, the
placebo effect is still one hell of a drug), reduce your
chances of murder by resisting the urge to have a huge
spread of species with demanding needs. I have found two
breeds which I personally find pleasing to look at, and are
very (very) low maintenance: money plants and painted-leaf
begonias. To populate my space, instead of going out and

buying new houseplants, I propagate the plants I already have (plant-boff code for a piss-easy way of making little plant babies – cut off a bit and stick it in an empty Coke can for a few weeks with water, then give it its own pot) and voila! A slowly growing army of plants that does not demand the money, time or energy it would require to learn how to care for a new species. They also make for great gifts: I have a grab and go approach to my window ledge for last-minute presents. Make sure you're reusing pots, using peat-free soil and look for plant swaps or exchanges in your local area. Buy new as a last resort.

EXPAND YOUR IDEA OF HOUSE CHORES

Remember that the floor your home is built on is potentially made of lava. If you're looking for excuses to rationalise spending less time on cleaning, decorating and polishing your home, here are a few things that I also consider home maintenance: campaigning for better flood defences in your county, getting involved in some community gardening, starting a WhatsApp group with your neighbours, learning about the local history around you and planning a walking tour for your friends, setting up a book swap box on your street. It's a much cheaper and less lonely way to spend your weekends, and you can still say 'sorry, I can't come, I've got chores to do.'

Now you're home and released from the grip of your domestic drudgery, it's probably time to have a shower and do some body admin, right?

Half-Arse Body

My relationship with my body is one of the most complicated I've ever been in. First off; it's an arranged marriage. Neither of us chose this, but, like it or lump it, we're stuck. She doesn't speak English, and she's an awful communicator – when I need a heart to heart, all she's got for me is a couple of mysteriously placed spots and a poorly timed mood swing.

I've heard that absence makes the heart grow fonder. While we've definitely craved some space from each other over the years, logistically that's off the table. Just as we start to get a rapport going, she'll change her tune and need different things.

We often have different ideas as to how a night out should go; she can't always keep up with my energy. There have been whole years of our marriage where I've stopped listening to her, sometimes bullied her about her appearance and generally been a bit of a dick. When I have tried to poison us with gin, she patiently ejects it from my mouth, eyes rolling. When she has wanted to jump the bones of a suspicious man, I have chucked her on the next train home with a cold compress. When I've been consistently clumsy, she grew us a cushion on our bum so we don't break our spine. She also has a prepper mentality and has always been obsessed with this 'famine' she's convinced is coming; so our 'home' is often cluttered with spare reserves I'm pretty sure we'll never use.

It's a battle of wills, it's an uneasy double act, but it's for life. I'm not even sure if the 'till death do us part' applies here. I guess we both go down with the worms?

Anyway, if this is all sounding vaguely familiar, if you have an enemies-to-lovers-to-amicable-roommates story arc with your own flesh prison, this chapter is for you. We're not out to make you live for ever, transform you into an Olympian, or give you the skin of a toddler. I'm not even going to ask you to #LOVEYOURSELF. Instead, we'll look at half-arsing as a way to be gentle with yourself in a world that wants you to be rigorous. Let's tip up your body to-do list and see what weird beliefs fall out, starting with the most dreaded . . .

GETTING YOUR ARSE UP (THE TYRANNY OF THE MORNING ROUTINE)

You rise at 5 a.m. The world feels new. You do a full Ashtanga yoga session followed by three litres of ice water from your charcoal-activated water bottle, which you prepped the night before with three slices of fresh organic lemon plucked from a grove in Sicily. Then you write out your 'morning pages' in your bespoke leather bullet journal, using a fountain pen personalised with your initials and loaded with organic ink in 'Imperial Blue'. After that it's time to activate your guided meditation app, the dulcet tones of your favourite celebrity whispering breathing techniques into your ear. Round it off with a rolled chia seed crumpet adorned with a complex assortment of yogurt and fruits, served on a piece of reclaimed Welsh slate.

I am suspicious of 99 per cent of the recommended morning routines out there. First off, notice the presence of multiple purchasable products and the absence of what we all know is missing: a really big morning poo.

Faecal habits aside, there are also many other considerations missing from the 'ideal' morning routines touted by wellness gurus and lifestyle influencers alike. To make time for the long list of rituals required to 'get your day started right', you must forfeit your sleep and rise hours before you usually would. Fear not though; in exchange for less time in bed (bed is for lazy people anyway, right?) you can glean the following benefits from being up with the larks and following their ideal activities:

Boost your immune system
Regulate your blood sugar levels
Balance your hormones
Improve your memory recall
Process your emotions
Uplift your mental wellbeing
De-escalate your anxiety
Cleanse toxic proteins that can result in Alzheimer's

checks notes Oh no, sorry, my mistake. That is *not* a list of things science can guarantee you will get from activities like journaling and ice baths and early mornings. That's a list of things you will gain when you sleep for longer.

The minimum advised sleep we all need is between seven and nine hours a night. For almost everyone, it's non-negotiable. It feels strange that, in a world where most people are getting under seven hours a night on average already, a genre of lifestyle advice would surface that is actually advising us to sleep *less* while trying to sell us back the benefits our body is willing to give us for free. I imagine the drawback for them is that we can't shop while unconscious.

Like millions of people, I've been radicalised to defend my right to sleep by sleep researcher Matthew Walker, who has written extensively about his findings around human snoozing and the dangers of letting anyone take it away from you. His work makes for a convincing read and has made me realise that many of the people in history who have been celebrated for their strict and short sleep cycles (Benjamin Franklin, Henry David Thoreau, Ronald Reagan, Winston Churchill and Margaret Thatcher to name a few) might not be the great poster children for early rising that some people think they are. While I can agree that, without a doubt, all those figureheads got things done, were those things good things? Were they in their best headspace? Did they always act with their reason intact? Results may vary.

There is a long list of things we apparently lack that it is promised will be restored to us with a morning routine: time to spend with ourselves, to mentally heal and prepare for the day, to look after our bodies, to prepare food that will nourish us. These are all noble ventures and I don't deny that they sound like things we *all* deserve. I'm just not sure turning to our sleep schedule to reimburse the time deficit should be our first instinct; rather it should be our last resort. Not to sound dramatic, but insufficient sleep is cited as a precursor to suicidal thoughts, it pushes your blood pressure up, it negatively impacts your heart rate, it increases your risk of infection, cardiovascular disease, anxiety, Alzheimer's, immunocompromisation, depression and even early death. *I know, right?!*

The modern world has us buzzing about around the clock, with little wiggle room for reflection or damage control. A morning routine feels like a great hack to this problem – simply MAKE MORE TIME by getting up earlier, you great lazy so-and-so!

The problem with that is that all shortcuts have consequences, and we deserve to know what they are before we proceed. We need to be reminded that, if at all possible, we should be asking for this time back from other parts of our life, not from our sleep schedule.

Some people are trapped in lives that necessitate a stretched schedule. That's the reality, and for those with no room for rearranging, we should fight for them to have better support. But if you are *not* trapped in a life where you have no options, don't let the world convince you to play pretend that you are. If you're at a stage where you're choosing whether to build a life where you'll be pushing your resources to their limits, or to build a life where you might also be able to get some regular sleep, take a look back at that list of consequences. It might well be worth your life to pick the job, or the partner, or the house that will make sure you don't have to cut into your seven to nine hours unless you absolutely need to.

Still want to have time to do yoga, journal, prepare healthy food? Instead of sacrificing sleep, perhaps it's time to have the hard conversations, to ask the people in your life if they can do the dog walk, or the nappies, or the batch-cook, or whatever it is that is keeping you from occasionally being able to do those desirable morning things that should not be squeezed into the ungodly hours. Ask for more time alone in the waking hours, if that's what you need. Quit the obligations that can be jilted, that need quitting, that clear the way for the time you need to take care of a human body, which is not as casual a feat as they would have you believe. And if you can't jilt them, get half-arsing, for the sake of your forty winks.

I absolve you of the moral obligation to rise early. Rise, if your body wriggles and wants to move. Fill your mornings with whatever makes you feel as though the world might not be awful. Drink too much coffee and let it race your mind over blank plains towards strange new ideas. Stretch if you feel achy, not because you're training to become a world-famous contortionist. Waste time winding yarn, or painting your nails, or doing a puzzle you will later crumble up, and know that it was not really wasted. And, if not, sleep. The scientists have your back.

MOVING YOUR ARSE (EXERCISE LIKE YOU BARELY CARE)*

In this next section, we're going to chat in more depth about bodies, health and calories. It's all positive but if you'd like to skip it, we'll see you on page 205.

Tragically I have to report, despite my best efforts, I have been unable to prove that exercise is bad for you. It would give me the greatest relief to strike it off my to-do list and tell you that it's fine to completely ditch it, but sadly the scientists persist in publishing brilliant peer-reviewed evidence to the contrary. We definitely need to be arsed, just a little bit – but it might not be the kind of arse-whipping you think it has to be. We don't have to go 'all in' to get something out of it and becoming a superhuman athlete is in no way necessary. We also don't need a huge amount of time, or money or even a routine. What we *do* desperately need is to simplify our relationship with exercise, starting with the name.

Exercise.

For me, the word makes clinical something that should be fun, or at least a bit of a relief. When someone says 'exercise' to me, images flash behind my eyelids of men in mesh tops kissing their biceps, lines of militant women on Peloton bikes, people looking like the light had died behind their eyes as they drop for 'one more' burpee. You might see your own dank school gym, smell the ridicule and Lynx Africa in the air, taste the incoming humiliation on your tongue. A collective shudder ripples through almost all of us when we hear the word 'exercise' and I fear that there simply isn't *time* to rectify that.

I'm all for reclaiming words but with the limited bandwidth we have there are probably more important words to defend. Instead, I'd like to half-arse it and choose some different, fresher replacements for 'exercise' that actually make us *want* to move. Let's throw some out there, I'll start:

How much more appealing does it sound to say,

'I'm off on a carcass march, want to come?'

or

'I'm taking my bones for walkies, back soon.'

or

'I'm off for a wiggle round the racetrack.'

or

'God, I'm so stressed, I really need a posterior voyage.'

Regardless of the name, it seems that NOT moving at all might lead to boring, unpleasant and time-consuming things in the future, like doctor's appointments and research and waiting for buses and filling out forms. Life will likely deal us enough of those ailments regardless of our work ethic, that's the roll of the dice of having a body, so if we can cut down on the likelihood of creating more, where possible, then that's a long-term half-arse win in my book. The strategy is to half-arse now to avoid having to be incredibly arsed later.

The good news is, that's all the effort you really *need*. Here are three reasons why . . .

HALF-ARSING IT WILL MAKE YOU HEALTHIER

When it comes to the long-term health benefits of exercise, it doesn't seem to be about how hard you train, or the type of movement you do; just that you keep it up over a long period of time. *The First 20 Minutes* by Gretchen Reynolds is a deep dive into how you can practically apply the science behind movement; its main takeaway being that almost all of the mortality reductions and health benefits associated with exercise can be attributed to the first twenty minutes of your workout. Everything after that doesn't really pack much of a punch. In fact, most benefits of exercise are 'curvilinear' – simply starting and doing a little bit raises the 'profits' astronomically, compared to not doing anything at all. As you do more, the gains level off, and actually drop if you overdo it. Our bodies are also very forgiving; most people maintain their strength gains for up to eight months after building them up, even if they start only putting in a third of the effort they had been previously. That 'January Rush' to the gym isn't actually recommended. Most evidence suggests that to avoid injury you shouldn't increase your training volume by more than 10 per cent a week. Starting slow and half-arsing it is where it's at, science says so.

That also applies to the frequency of movement too; skipping a workout is not the sin a lot of fitness gurus would have us believe. The general advice from most experts is that 150 minutes of *light to moderate* exercise every week is ideal and your body categorically *doesn't care* how you split that up, or whether you 'beat your best' or not. Twenty minutes a day of brisk walking? Great! Two seventy-five-minute gym sessions? Fine! Half an hour of moderate living room boogies on a weekday? Deal! Our bodies are easier to please than we think. I only wish that we'd stop painting them as these complicated, demanding overlords because they're actually more aligned with the mentality of a bouncy dog who simply wants to go on a walk around the block with us.

HALF-ARSING IT WILL MAKE YOU SMARTER

As it turns out, the jock/geek paradigm that plays out in all my favourite nineties rom-coms is a bit flawed. Movement is actually one of the key factors in stimulating neurogenesis (a fancy way of describing the process that creates new brain cells), meaning that at least some of those background characters on the football team could probably *also* lay down a mean algebraic formula. Every day, it seems, more research comes out showing the positive impact exercise wields over brain function, and it's something I'm a little pissed I didn't know about earlier; especially the influence of exercise on our working memory. The cognitive scientist Dr Sian Beilock describes it as the 'scratch pad' of our brains, roughly sketching out the workings of whatever problem our brain is trying to solve. Stress can reduce our working memory's capacity, but exercise can jump-start it; and those with a smaller working memory benefit the most from short, moderate bouts of exercise. On top of better problem-solving, exercise can also give us a good boost of dopamine, useful for creativity, focus, control of movement (great for the clumsy) and for being able to remain positive.

It makes sense when you think that the structure of the human brain was formed during lives packed with activity: hunter-gatherers were often on the move and much less stationary than us. When we move, even just a little, we're creating the kind of rhythm our brains were designed to thrive in.

HALF-ARSING IT WILL ACTUALLY MAKE IT HAPPEN

When I first started running, I had an app that would measure how far and how fast I managed to do it, to the centimetre . . . I thought it would motivate me, or at least give me a measure of whether my runs were actually 'good ones'. Instead, it just made me feel like a failure when my run was, because of my pace or distance, considered 'below average' on the app. Which was silly when you think about it, because my aim had never been to be GOOD at running, only to run. I have since deleted the app since it turns out **ALL RUNS ARE GOOD RUNS.**

A lot of the 'helpful' tips around any movement habit include a focus on optimisation, metrics and progress. They want very specific things from you: miles, reps, laps. Understandably perhaps, as they're designed for people who want to FOCUS on fitness. The problem was, I wasn't someone who wanted to focus on fitness. I just wanted it to be a footnote; an *essential* footnote, but I wasn't looking to become good at it. I just wanted those long-term benefits and for my legs not to fall off through disuse. I was looking to go from 'not doing it' to 'being rubbish at it'. At least then I'd be doing it. Maybe 'rubbish at it' was all I could manage, as I'd already allocated my arses elsewhere, but it was a damn sight better than not moving my arse at all.

After several failed attempts (see above reasons), I am finally a 'regular' runner. I run about three times a week. And I did it by caring very little about the outcomes. My only rules were: leave the house, in your running shoes, don't return for at least twenty minutes. Walking the whole way was allowed. Sometimes I did that, but it meant getting bored pretty easily, and soon I ran little spurts purely to avoid the tedium. Wearing running gear outdoors in England without running is mostly, as it turns out, pretty cold, so sometimes I'd move a bit just because it was MORE comfortable to jog. Eventually I found a route that I liked and felt safe running through, and now I simply run that same route whenever I can. It took a few months of pounding that route before I looked up its distance. Three kilometres was a nice surprise, but I resisted the urge to start timing how long it took me, or to elongate the route. Sometimes I'll feel like doing more, sometimes a little less. Both are allowed because I've realised the most important thing is to not return to the house with a negative recent memory of running. That is the no. 1 biggest predictor of whether I break a habit or not. If my last memory of it is miserable, if I pushed myself too hard or return soaked by rain, my subconscious will kick and resist next time my running shoes look at me in that 'come hither' way. You'll often overhear fitness-boffs boast that they don't consider themselves in competition with others, only with themselves. It's their personal best they're trying to beat, not the others around them. I say: why bother? Let's take that attitude one step further; why be in competition with yourself? Stop competing altogether and focus on what your body can do right now. A dog who is deep in 'walkies' isn't comparing his frolicking speed to his performance yesterday, or worrying if he's keeping up with last week's trotting time. Not bothering with improvement or exponential growth has been my key to actually keeping exercise up. I've allowed myself to believe that it's for fun.

As much as I am sceptical about many aspects of the best-selling book *Atomic Habits*, one concept from those pages does make a lot of sense: habit stacking. In this concept, James Clear advises attaching a habit that you'd like to start doing to one you already do. So, if you want to remember to take your tablets, 'attach' it to the habit of brushing your teeth and train your brain to do it straight after. If you want to write once a week, why not get into the habit of doing it straight after taking out the bins, etc.

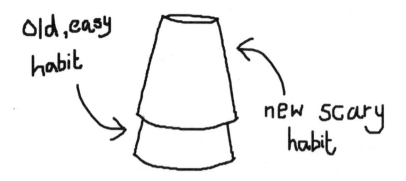

Old, easy habit

new scary habit

A few years ago I glued my habit of showering (pretty frequent) to my very ropey 'habit' of jogging (very infrequent). The idea was: every time I needed a shower, I'd try to make time for a twenty-minute jog beforehand. Do I always do this? Absolutely not. But it has resulted in me running several times a week, which, even at my fail rate, is MUCH higher than it was before The Great Stacking. It doesn't mean that if I'm tired or it's dark or I simply can't be arsed I force myself to run before I wash; only that, every time I get a whiff of my armpits and think 'I should probably have a shower' there is an auto button in my brain that plays the question 'could I squeeze a run in first?'. As someone who never thinks about running unprompted, and to whom the idea would otherwise rarely occur, this is a very basic, silly kind of magic.

HALF-ARSING IS LESS EFFORT THAN YOU THINK

Of course, not everyone's bodies or brains are keen on running and that's totally fine. It's not for everyone. It's not possible for everyone. That doesn't mean a good habit-stacked half-arse movement isn't for you. Our hyperfocus on

weight loss or completely 'able' bodies or superhuman
performance neglects to tell the tale of how beneficial small
actions can be. From joint health to mental wellbeing and
cardiovascular disease, there are lots of invisible ways our
bodies can be suffering or thriving, and there's simply no
way of knowing by looking at them. Todd M. Manini
studied the impact of exercise on people's daily expenditure
of energy and how it could predict their chances of being
alive a decade down the line. He found that on average, for
every 287 calories extra burned, your chances of early
mortality can go down by 30 per cent. To give you an idea,
doing laundry, gardening or vacuuming can burn a couple of
hundred calories an hour. You can double your metabolic
rate by simply strolling around at about one and a half to
two miles an hour, which is the speed we tend to go when
we're shopping. In the 'fitness' world, those numbers would
be deemed rookie; but if you're willing to be slap-dash about
it, if you'd just like to stay alive a bit longer and be a bit
more healthy, these small half-arsed gestures can
literally be life-lengthening.

These kinds of low-effort movements that can even include
stirring a pot of food as you cook and fidgeting your leg up
and down as you sit, have a whole field of research
surrounding them and their benefits, named 'non-exercise
activity thermogenesis', or NEAT for short. They're purported
to have huge health benefits, so, you see, you might not be
arsing up movement as badly as you think. Even the famous
advice of getting in 10,000 steps a day is a little bogus. Long
story short, that number was plucked from the air by a
Japanese pedometer manufacturer in the 1960s without any
research to back it up. Ten thousand was simply chosen

because it was an easy number to remember. Research has since proven that the health benefits of taking steps drop off at around 7,000–8,000 steps, anything in excess of that is great, but has been shown to have diminishing returns.

Building more movement into the things you already do won't give you any cool pictures to flex with on social media, but can be as effective as any light gym habit and much cheaper. When shopping online I choose pick-up points for my parcels that are further away from my house than the one the website suggests. I book the hairdresser in the next town over from me and walk. I've stopped doing weekly food shops so I have to get up and walk to the shops more often (also great for reducing food waste). Your half-arse movement might look different to mine, but I bet there are ways you can build a little more gallivanting into your own life. Perhaps you get off the bus a few stops early or only take calls standing up. Instead of stacking plates at the same time after you've finished the washing up, cross the kitchen each time to put each one away individually. Or, when you're unloading groceries, place your shopping bags in another room and put each item away one at a time. Walk around the room during the ad-breaks of your favourite TV programme. Nothing is too silly in my book. If you have both an upstairs and a downstairs bathroom at home or at work, make a rule that you have to use the one that's on the other floor when you need to go. Instead of catching up with friends in a café, take your coffees on walks around parks or your local area. In Jane Austen's day they called this 'taking a turn about the gardens' and it doubled as a great excuse to get away from rude men, boring neighbours and to bitch, away from prying ears, about vicars you don't want to marry. So, to honour her, try that.

HOW TO MAKE HALF-ARSE MOVING HAPPEN

1. Find something involving movement that you don't mind doing. Experiment for as long as you need to. It can be a common thing like running, but it can be as weird or as 'unexercisey' as you like. Dance breaks in your living room or in toilet stalls at work count.

2. Make a list of things you do or places you go every day or every week. Can you tag-team some movement onto any of those?

3. Control for over-optimism. Set a rough idea of how regularly you'd like to do it, and then HALVE THAT RATE.

4. Define your own terms for 'done it'. Don't set a performance goal. Do not measure how fast, or how well, you do it. Attendance goals are what we're looking for, just like at school. Turning up.

5. Do not, under any circumstances, sign up for a marathon.

6. Make sure you end on a good memory; if that means stopping before you're exhausted or really uncomfortable, great.

7. DO NOT tell yourself you're arsing it up.

BORING BUT PISS-EASY WAYS TO BE SLIGHTLY HEALTHIER WITHOUT REALLY TRYING

WATCHING YOUR ARSE

This wasn't intentional when I started my quest to study the spirit of 'arse' in all its academic and metaphorical contexts, but allegorically our arses stand in for a lot.

> *'I hate his arse!'*
>> *'They're a pain in the arse!'*
>>> *'She is kickass!'*
>>> *'He better watch his arse!'*

In these contexts, an 'arse' stands in for a whole person. You *are* your arse. So imagine my surprise and sense of universal synergy when I do some digging and realise that, without our literal physical arses, we are nothing.

Our back is the most vital part of the structure of our body, and what supports the back? The butt. Pains and injuries in your neck, hips, knees, lower back and even your ankles can be traced back to a weak bum, and healed with the strength of a strong one. By strengthening our bums, not only can we prevent injury on a structural level, but it can also improve our balance. If you're naturally clumsy like me, having fewer wobbles and being able to NOT fall over when you inevitably walk into that thing you thought was further away than it actually is, can also prevent those unexpected and deeply mortifying injuries.

If you're struggling to master a sport, investing in your butt might be your most effective, efficient gameplan – stability in your hips is the best way to change direction effectively and precisely. So, whether you're swinging a golf club, kicking a ball or swimming a lap, you will need the cooperation of your bum.

Fellow hunchers, our bums might be what is standing between us and good alignment: modern desks and ways of sitting can lead to weak and 'sleepy' glutes, giving us a really poor basis from which to be able to stay sitting up straight for long periods of time.

In even better news, you can get all of these health benefits without having to ALSO work towards a nice-looking butt. You can't tell the muscle density from looking at an arse, or measuring its size or shape. The 'nice butts' you see online might not actually be as healthy as you imagine them to be. Especially if they're the result of a butt lift, which is, ironically, actually *very bad* for your butt health.

If you're not into lifting weights or doing full-body muscle toning but you do want to reap *some* of the long-term benefits of muscle building, your half-arse focus can simply be . . . your arse. I have never (and probably will never) set aside time to specifically work out my glutes. Instead, with what little patience I have for muscle building, I try to do a few squats whenever I'm boiling the kettle (which is often; I knew my tea addiction was good for something) or brushing my teeth. You can pick your mundane task of choice to accompany a little bum work and scratch *'glutes? work on?'* off your list.

THE MAGIC OF INTENTIONAL LEFTOVERS

I'm often stuck between a rock and a hard place when it comes to the moralities of home-cooking. 'The rock' being the people who seem to cook from scratch for every meal, eat it straight away and glow from within as they do it. 'The hard place' being the people who have the mental capacity to plan their food a week in advance and meal-prep like they're trying out for a spot in the Marines. I have long ago accepted that I'm capable of neither on a regular basis, but I've recently been comforted by the research around the nutritional advantages of leftovers. Did you know that when starch is cooked in water and then cooled, it restructures itself? And then again when you reheat it? According to research at the University of Surrey, assisted by the BBC, reheated pasta, potato and other starchy carbs are much better for you once they've cooled down, and even more so when they're reheated. Whilst your blood sugars can spike after a hot, fresh meal, the transformed starch you get from leftovers can ease those spikes, give you all the benefits of fibre, generally improves digestion, leaves beneficial bacteria in your gut . . . all without you having to make any change to what you're eating. Think of it as reverse meal-prepping.

I can also attest that things like bolognese, brownies and marinated tofu all taste MUCH better once they've been left to sit in the fridge for a day or two, so, really, you're upgrading your whole menu.

Whilst the meal-preppers might have the aesthetic high ground, with their fancy Tupperware marked with all the days of the week, simply getting into the habit of cooking double or triple quantities on those days when you *do* have the energy to cook will give you all the cost-saving, home-cooked benefits of meal-prepping, without having to have any of the foresight. And it might do your gut some good too.

DON'T KICK YOUR COFFEE HABIT, JUST REARRANGE IT

I *cannot* be arsed to 'be sensible' and regulate my caffeine intake to the nth degree; a little coffee is such a wonderful, tiny joy in my life. Spending a lot of energy trying to kick a relatively harmless habit doesn't appeal to me. I have, however, after some research, made a tiny tweak to my habit that has made a huge difference: I have my first coffee of the day AFTER I have breakfast, never before. Studies have shown that, especially after the sort of disrupted night of sleep that makes you turn to coffee immediately after you rise, coffee on an empty stomach followed by breakfast decreases our chance of being able to metabolise the glucose in our food by around 50 per cent. When we can't process glucose properly, it ends up being released into our blood all at once, rather than slowly being released by our liver over a longer period of time. It's also worth knowing that it's not *necessarily* a bad thing to be a bit groggy in the morning; over the course of the first hour you're awake, your body is trying to clear out the 'sleepy chemical' adenosine that it flooded you with the night before to make sure you went to sleep. Messing with that natural process by waking yourself up with caffeine, before the body is ready to process it, can lead to a big crash once the caffeine's effects wear off. Reaching for a bit of water and a massive bowl of cereal with blueberries when I first rise not only distracts me from making eyes at my coffee jar, but wakes my body up enough so that when I *do* hit it with some caffeine, it's ready to rock and roll. Think of it as a surprise visit from a close friend; it's not that you don't love greeting them at the door, but the welcome will be MUCH warmer if they turn up at 8 a.m. rather than 7. That's how your body feels about caffeine.

ARSE-SESS THE WAY YOU SIT

Spending ages doing yoga and getting deep-tissue massages is great, but not possible/fun for everyone. I am chuffed if I get to one yoga class a month. What has changed my life (with very little effort) is working out WHY I'm feeling all the aches and pains. Fix that arrangement once and feel the benefits for ever. For me mine was my lower back. I did some research and realised that humans weren't really designed to sit for long periods of time with their knees level with their hips. I got myself a kneeling chair and, when I don't have access to that, I make sure I sit a little forward in a normal seat, with my feet tucked behind me, lowering my knees. It's weird and outrageous and so simple and I'm furious it works, but it does. Guilt about not doing morning yoga, eliminated. Now you can just do it if you fancy it, rather than feeling like it's a medical emergency. Your ache-source might be different, but it's worth spending a little time looking at what is causing that discomfort, so that you can half-arse the time remedying it and muck about instead.

Now we've stopped fretting about our step count and our meal prep, we're off to the bathroom cabinets to see what horrors lie within . . .

ARSE OVER FACE (SKINCARE)

The world of skincare is a $186 billion industry, which will either shock you or make you shrug and go 'sounds about right'. For anyone who has gotten this far and doesn't understand why we must spend the next few pages discussing face cream: it sounds like you have your arses in order. Stay innocent and feel free to skip. This phenomenon hasn't reached everybody, and thank goodness.

As someone who has been suckered into parting with serious dosh in exchange for little bottles of liquid luck, I would like to cover the appeals of the skincare industrial complex, for anyone reading who doesn't 'get' the allure of the 'skincare routine'.

Sometimes, the world can feel like a relentless game of Whac-A-Mole. There are annoying little gophers popping up everywhere: queue-pushers, soup-slurpers, teething offspring, impatient bosses, bad parkers, sulky spouses. The little hammer the world hands us to fend off these torments can feel feeble in the face of all that chaos.

BUT when everything else fails, we can twist the lid off our personal apothecary and kneed out the fraught smiles and furrowed brows of the day. We can feel like we did something right. We skin-*CARED*. We PRESERVED something. We stuck to a ROUTINE. We didn't entirely let ourselves down, despite all temptations to. Unlike makeup (fun but spirals down the plug hole come nightfall), skincare *feels* like an investment; like we're building up exponential gains, something that will show real returns. It's a potion, a plot against a world that wants to see us decay; it's magic, but it's also something better. It's science. It's got science words on the bottle. It says 'clinically proven' on the side. As I shut the lid of my night cream I whisper: *'women in STEM!'*

With all that satisfaction (or the promise of it) comes the guilt. Am I missing a step? Am I doing it in the right order? Will I pay with my skin for buying the cheaper bottle? Does everyone know an ingredient that I don't?

Having a skincare routine is a time commitment, no doubt about it. It's not just in the application of this regime, but the hours spent researching which products are 'correct', wandering aisles squinting at labels and sniffing at samples, earning the money to pay for it. All of this puts skincare high in the 'arse commitment' ranking and makes it worthy of a closer look. Especially because often there is an implied 'laziness' behind not participating. Apparently, on average, women spend about two and a half hours a week on their skincare routine.

Someone recently congratulated me on my bravery for 'showing my skin' on social media, as though my skin was a pile of clutter in the background of my camera frame I could have stuffed into a drawer or swept under a carpet. My first thought was 'do I have a choice? I'm covered in the stuff?' but a moment later I realised that the commenter must have been exposed to so many people online who were using filters to alter their skin, that the view of mine, in the binary, became 'brave'. I had a flash of a memory from a skincare shop years before, where the shop assistant asked me if my skin was 'dry', 'oily' or 'combination', as though skin could only be 'broken' in one way or another, or in both. I asked if there was a fourth option, 'neither'? Her expression was all the reply I needed.

For those who live with medically serious cases of acne or eczema, our constant chatter about skincare solutions must be frustrating. I think there's been a large-scale equating of medical conditions that show up on the skin and 'unfavourable' visual quirks of normal skin that we apply medical terminology to. My red blotches don't need to be 'changed'; they need to be 'treated'. My pores aren't simply functional or not; they are assessed on size; it is suggested that I shrink them. Products are packaged in medicinal-looking bottles, often paid for at 'counters' that mimic pharmacies, and (worst of all) occasionally sold to us by shop assistants in lab coats. The great pantomime of the skincare theatrical tradition is endearing, until it starts tempting you to hand over more time and money than you were planning on committing to a face that looked fine ten minutes ago before you crossed their threshold.

Conveniently, there are as many solutions as there are potential problems, all with a hefty price tag. One survey found that appearance-related spending is costing women $225,000 per lifetime, with almost a quarter being shelled out on our faces. If we guess that we spend fifty years of our lives having both money and the will to spend it on face maintenance, that's about £85 a month. The best-selling skincare products I frequently spot range in price between £20–£100, and that's for products aimed at the average, pharmacy-dwelling consumer. Don't even cross the threshold of the higher-end skincare brands if you're not willing to part with some serious wads of cash.

So, is it a load of old arse? Well, I did some digging and I'm here to relieve you of your duties as medical matron of your own skin. When it comes to cleaning, your skin is already on it, there's no need to create a large amount of extra admin. Your skin is constantly detoxing. It's why Botox needs to be redone regularly – because the body is literally flushing it out as a *toxin*. Exfoliating products promise to take off the 'dead' skin cells so that you can see the newer ones below it – that's actually a good idea, SUCH a good idea that our bodies invented it millennia ago. It's continually rebuilding the surface of the skin, in cycles lasting around a month. As for all the cells in your body? According to the *New Scientist*, none them are older than around fifteen and a half years. Now how's that for a comforting anti-ageing thought?!

As for the rest? The anti-aging, the plumping, the rejuvenating? There are individual '#science' reasons why each one has shown very little evidence for actually working, but in the broadest strokes most can be explained this way: the skin has scaffolding in it, the structures that keep its shape. The better the scaffolding, the less wrinkled and more plump the skin. The scaffolding has stuff in it with names like 'elastin' and 'collagen'. ABOVE the scaffolding is a very cool barrier, a top layer, that fancy people call the 'stratum corneum'. It's basically the big bad bodyguard, it's designed not to be messed with. Tiny problem – if you want to

IMPROVE the scaffolding of your skin, you have to (slightly ironically) mess with the structure that is designed to preserve it. You have to get through that barrier. Luckily, your bodyguard doesn't give a flying fig how much you spent on that serum. Hyaluronic Acid? Nope. Extra collagen? No chance. Dr Szu S. Wong, lecturer in pharmaceutical studies at Keele University in the UK described it as like trying to squeeze 'an elephant through a cat flap'. It is theoretically possible to get through if you are a VERY tiny molecule; you could sneak through the fatty 'mortar' between the 'brick' cells, but you have to be fat-soluble to do that, which even excludes the much-adored anti-ageing powerhouse ingredient, vitamin C (even L'Oréal admit it has a very low level of penetration into the skin).

One treatment I thought would be marginally easier to defend was retinoids (or vitamin A derivatives; like common, over-the-counter 'essentials' retinal or retinol) but while they might have *some* effects for *some* people, there are shockingly few public studies to back up the claims boldly printed on retinol bottles. One of the best and most thorough studies of the claims retinoid manufacturers make had this to say after their very extensive inspection: 'there is very little, if any, trustworthy evidence available to support the use of over-the-counter cosmetic retinol-containing products to improve the appearance of aged skin.'

Ouch.

The stronger, prescription-only type of vitamin A, tretinoin or 'tret' does offer a few more positive signs of, perhaps, working, but for most of us who don't require medical interventions and just want to see fewer lines, its impact remains dubious.

In fact, when you look at the evidence produced by manufacturers to back up the claims they make on behalf of their skincare products, mostly it simply looks like they can't be arsed; very few use control groups, or factor in placebo effects. Now that I've read them, I can't unsee all of the caveats used in claims about the skincare products we know and love. For instance, 'clinically proven' isn't a regulated term for cosmetics in the way that it is for drugs; something can be 'clinically proven' if you test it on one billion people, or simply *one person*. So, when a label says '100 per cent of women say their skin looked firmer', it could well be one woman named Janet who smothered the chemical equivalent of mashed banana on her face and simply 'felt' like she looked like the cat's pyjamas.

In even worse news, some evidence suggests that ingredients in modern skincare can actually make the signs of ageing worse. Writer and researcher Jessica DeFino explains: 'the research shows that the more we put on our skin in terms of external topical products, the more we disrupt the skin barrier and disrupt the skin microbiome, which are basically the two things you need to have intact in order to have skin that functions on its own.'

WHAT TO BE ARSED WITH

So, what DOES make my skin look better? For most 'ailments', the answers are usually the cheapest and most boring: water, exercise, sleep, vegetables. If, however, what you care about most is preventing the signs of ageing, to find the most effective answer you'll have to get your arse out.

No, I'm serious.

If you look at the skin on your bum, you will see the skin YOUR body has the ability to produce, if you left it in a dark room all the time. Looks smooth and unwrinkled, right? The skin on your bum (I presume) has never been given specialist treatment, been smeared with retinoids or been given an ingredient-ridden mask. The only specialist treatment your bum has been given is peace and quiet. A life away from the tyranny of the sun. If your arse is anything like mine, it's been living the blissful life of a budgie under a blanket, in almost total darkness, apart from the occasional hit of daylight from an ill-advised victory flash after climbing a mountain (guilty) or that one time you might have forgotten to close the curtains during day-sex (not me, sir, no). Apart from that, the most light it's seen is the glow of indoor lamps or occasionally a cheeky string of fairy lights.

The number one cause of aging skin is *daylight*. Ergo, the only form of true, scientific, peer-reviewed, highly-likely-they're-not-lying anti-aging gear on the market is . . . SPF.

The only other thing you could *safely* throw your money at that would *guarantee* you a reduction in the future formation of wrinkles would be pre-purchasing and climbing into your own coffin early, lying there in the dark and employing a butler to hand you food and water through a hatch until you die. Apart from making my death more logistically practical for my loved ones, this one doesn't have much appeal for me.

You do you, I'd never yuck someone else's yum, but I choose SPF.

This was a short section but that is because this is a short answer. How refreshing! Get some regular SPF on you and you've done all the arsing you really need to!

Okay, I lied; there is a second component that makes up the true solution to skincare. It's that part of the chapter where we look down at the lava. There are four main types of exposure that can arse-up your skin: pollution, light, climate, irritants. If you squint you'll be able to see the fine print in that statement . . .

Pollution (caused by fossil-fuelled industries, over-consumption and inefficient transport)

Light (an abundance of which is caused by a thinning ozone layer)

Climate (rapidly changing due to the fossil fuel industry)

Irritants (otherwise known as chemicals, usually extracted in ways that are unsafe to humans and the environment)

An increase in air pollution and the ever-increasing ultraviolet radiation from the sun means that we're forced to try to apply, as best we can, a protective barrier to substitute the one the earth is rapidly losing. All this to say, skincare is not a *you* problem, it's an *us* problem. And the longer we spend arsing around in the aisles of Boots trying to buy liquid luck, the less time we'll have to march for something better. What do we want? A just transition into green energy (with a glowing complexion thrown in at no extra cost or effort)! When do we want it? Yesterday!

HALF-ARSE SKINCARE STRATEGIES

Half-arse skin strategies to put in your bathroom cabinet:

SPF Slathering

Buy a good (I didn't say expensive) SPF for your face. Use it every day. Not a spray, that spreads it out, you need a good cream slather, and to rub it in. Not as part of a foundation or a makeup product. Just the raw, strong, good stuff. Two finger lengths is the recommended amount. Yeah, I know, more than you thought, right? Congratulations, you're off the hook. You have now done the only science-backed step towards anti-ageing. And even if you're not bothered about the wrinkles, SPF's anti-cancer properties should inspire you to keep slathering.

If you can't see it, don't solve it

Still tempted to spend time and money researching skincare? This is my half-arse test to see whether any given skin ailment is something that actually matters to me. Without cheating, can I list ANYONE from my friendship group that I have noticed this skin 'ailment' on? If I cannot detect it on others, and it poses no real health risk, then it's out.

Fun first

STILL feel heartbroken at the idea of giving up your skincare routine? That's totally fine! As long as you accept and celebrate that the joys of skincare are largely about the tactile experience of the routine itself, rather than the results, I see no harm here. Enjoy the colours

213

of the bottles, the smells, the temporary softness. After my deep dive into the skincare paperwork, I've promised myself that if I want to buy any products again, I'll only get the stuff whose ratio of price point to joy-level is such that if it turned out they DIDN'T work and were just a con, I would shrug and say 'well, I had a good time.'

Touch that face!

Skincare doesn't need to be your excuse to give yourself a face massage. It's your body heat and touch senses that make it worthwhile, so use any cream or face oil you like, cheap as chips. My favourite habit is treating myself to a little eyebrow massage when I pop to the loo, after I've washed my hands and I'm just lingering by the mirror.

Hang out with yourself.

What did you really want out of this? If skincare, and indeed beauty rituals in general, are an attempt at embodiment, to ground ourselves in our own skin and remember that we're not just a brain in a jar . . . then there are tons of free and half-arse ways to do that. Skip the hours of Internet research and worrying about if you're using the right products (don't they tell us that worry creates frown lines? So why the stress-inducing advertising, eh?!) and try some easier ways of slipping back into your skin – what makes you feel at home in your body? What grounds you? What actually makes you breathe out in relief? Do more of that before you reach for the bottles.

Realise you're already doing it.

You are already doing skincare. Without even knowing it. If you drink water, eat fruit and vegetables, sleep adequately and occasionally move about, you're doing it. Those are things that can genuinely improve your skin, although there are a ton of other reasons to do them too. You've been multitasking this whole time, you clever clogs. Want to up the skincare? Up all of the things I mentioned above. Already doing lots of it? Consider the chore of skincare struck off the list.

Oh yeah, and lastly. . .
Start a revolution.

SKINCARE FOR YOUR BRAIN

At the end of the day, I can't be too mad because the clue was in the name. What was sold to me by the skincare industry as a 'beauty ritual' was exactly that: a ritual. A series of sincere steps we move through to *create* meaning. The wedding ceremony doesn't change the biology of your body or transform the chemistry of your heart; but undertaken willingly, with the full understanding of what it can achieve, and what you must build yourself, it can be a positive kind of ritual. If, however, you're marched to the altar to be married off to someone you don't enjoy, under the threat of not being worthy of love if you don't comply; well, that's a ritual that needs uprooting.

While there's nothing natural about skincare, there is something incredibly natural about fearing discrimination and wanting to protect yourself from that. Unfortunately, there's no cream that deflects judgement (but imagine how quickly it would fly off the shelves if there were). You have to have had a lot of advantages in life to be able to opt IN to skincare, and for some they feel like that advantage will be lost should they opt out. Only *you* can know what prompts you to slather on the snake oil, and whether it makes you feel subservient or subversive. For me, scaling back my skincare feels like the perfect half-arse way to save money, save time and, in some small way, stick it to a culture that fears ageing more than it fears death. Which is ironic, because wrinkles are literally a sign that you haven't died; that you've lived past youth, and you're still kicking. Every new line on my face is an attendance tick: Leena turned up, yet again, despite it all.

In our defence, it makes sense to wonder if you should worry about your skin. Your skin is the biggest organ on your body, which might make you think 'well, maybe I should allocate it the most amount of time and care', but it might not need you as much as you think it does. It's already got systems in place to self-exfoliate, cleanse, moisturise and heal. Very rarely does it need any kind of serious intervention, or regular 'upkeep'. Much like a teenager that no longer needs to be fed, or watched, or entertained, and in fact gets enraged at any perceived interference (get out of my room, Mum!), human skin has been evolving just fine so far and, while it sometimes gets into a scrape, overall it's best left to mulch in its bedroom. It will come downstairs when it's ready.

LOVING YOUR ARSE

After all the struggle and strife that has gone into both my own and (perhaps) your 'journey' towards 'loving your body' it might seem strange to hear what I want to say next:

Don't bother.

I mean it. Don't bother.

Don't bother, because the body you sink hours into loving *now* will not be the same body in a few years and you'll have to start all over again. Don't bother, because bodies are there to be made use of more than they are there to be admired. Don't bother, because bodies don't respond well to being stared at, even if you're attempting to do it lovingly. Those hours are better spent hurling yourself down hills, covered in grass, or melting into a delicious dish of pasta.

Just like the morning routine, the quest for self-love has a really expensive gift shop. It is ready to sell you a lot of mugs, t-shirts, books, creams and expensive retreats. When something suspicious is being flogged for money at a large scale, it doesn't make me think 'wow, people are so gullible'. Instead, it's a really useful piece of data about how many people want something, and how desperately they want it.

There has never been a calm, normal time to 'come of age', but I think I was making the transition from child into adult at a particularly weird era of Western beauty standards. The beginning of my puberty was hailed in by openly fatphobic TV programmes like *What Not to Wear* and *The Biggest Loser* whilst an incredibly slender Martine McCutcheon was being cast as 'chubby' in *Love, Actually*. By the time my teenage years were drawing to a close, Caitlin Moran was touting short-and-dumpy body acceptance, I was ordering books with titles like *Fat Is a Feminist Issue* and everyone was pointing out that perhaps Bridget Jones was not the very useful plus-size icon we all had held her up to be. It was truly a decade of cultural whiplash.

From the mulch and acidity of white Western beauty standards rose rebellions quiet and loud. Whilst the Body Positive movement is an incredibly powerful grassroots anti-capitalist movement, made by and created for plus-size, racialised, disabled, queer bodies, its weird baby sister, the 'love yourself' brigade, has a few more merch items and a lot fewer ambitious demands for justice. While the political movement championing positivity around marginalised communities should be protected and advocated for at all possible moments, its co-opting has diluted its message and perhaps given those of us for whom it was not intended a false sense of having 'failed' if we don't look in the mirror and feel *gleeful* at the very sight of ourselves.

You might have already done the 'work' of learning to love how you look; or have loved your body all along. Good for you, no sarcasm intended. You might have, like me, sunk so many hours into reprogramming your brain into finding yourself 'hot' or 'attractive' after the barrage of media you consumed during your formative years, that you're starting to wonder whether you're trying to play the devil at his own game, and that maybe folding would be the real power move. The barrage of 'self-love' mantras and material can often feel like a stealthy way of attempting to do exactly what the media that got you into this mess did: brainwash you. Plant thoughts in your head that aren't your own. Try to make you override how you're feeling with a new file, rather than reading what is really there.

I spent so many years trying to honestly be able to answer the question 'am I beautiful?' with a wholehearted 'yes!' that I didn't stop to wonder whether the question was even relevant. If it should even matter to me.

Even if you are one of those people who have successfully mastered the art of 'loving themselves', dog ear this page, you might need it later. After all, bodies change. Loving a body is like loving a tide line; can it stay still long enough for you to truly know it? Probably not. But can you love the simple fact that it exists, that you can depend on it to return to you and beat rhythms against sand and be beautiful, whatever form it takes today? Yes.

I want to shout from the rooftops 'bodies are there to be used!' but I hate how the word 'used' has become synonymous with 'exploited'. Used in the best way, used by you and you alone, used as in: make use of, deploy, exert, WIELD. Wield is a great one. Wield your body because bodies move and make things and that's the coolest thing about them. No self-respecting kid is handed a set of paints or a football or a yo-yo and says: *do you know what, I think I'll just look at it.*

To try to assess how attractive you are is to set yourself the task of crawling inside the brains of everyone you will ever meet and deducing what makes them tick.

Nora Ephron says that 'love is homesickness'; in that you tend to fall in love with someone who reminds you of something you are homesick for, some qualities that feel in some way familiar, aspects of a face or a gesture or a foible that you hoped would return to you. It's why, in a completely non-Oedipal way, we sometimes accidentally end up with people who echo our parents, or a sibling, or an ex.

We can't predict the peculiarities of another person's taste, or what, in a stranger, they will find inexplicably familiar. To find a home in another person is not the same as finding the perfect pantone shade for the hallway, or one stylishly placed lamp. It's the mismatched collection of mugs in a cupboard, it's the feeling of leaving your muddy boots on the mat and not having to worry, the view from the bathroom window onto the tree that changes with the seasons but never uproots and walks off.

So many beauty treatments or body refinements are focused on smoothing and blurring. From forehead fillers to shapewear, the fixation is on removing the peaks and troughs of a silhouette or a profile, to flatten what has become unruly. The eye wrinkles or the cellulite, when reduced to a line, would go from this:

To this.

———————————————

Except, you'll notice something. This line is empty. It has no cadence.

In other circles, this kind of flat line would just be the base. In music, it's the stave, it's the silence that the music streaks itself on top of. In a voice recording, it's the tremor in the line that lets you know, without hearing anything, that someone is speaking.

In A&E, it's the wiggly line on the monitor that tells you someone is living.

If a body is a place to come home to, for you or the person you love, don't you want them to be able to recognise you from afar? Don't you want them to be able to pick you out of a line-up, spot you as they crest a mountain at dusk after a long journey, see your present self in your childhood pictures, be able to trace you like an etching, bumps and all?

Sorry to labour a point that could fast become hackneyed, but LUMPS AND BUMPS ARE THE VITAL SIGNS OF LIFE. They're what make you feel like home to others.

Just like a familiar living room, they're signs that you are LIVED IN. Instead of kicking off our shoes and feeling welcome in our own bodies, we seem to sit at the mirror that is hung in this liminal space between original and perfect and prod ourselves until we are neither.

THE 'SO WHAT IF I WAS?' GAME

What if, every time your mind says *I am ugly/unattractive/a minger*, you don't try to push it down with instant rebuttals of No, I'm not! *I am beautiful and perfect in every single way!*? What if, instead, you call its bluff?

What if you reply; *so what if I am? What is it that I don't think I deserve, if I'm 'ugly'?*

It's true that the world might withhold things from me, or treat me differently, if I was, by the world's standards, 'ugly'. But, if I believe that I deserve respect, resources and a good time regardless of how I look, then if I don't get those things because of 'being ugly', that wouldn't be my fault, would it? Too often I find that my inner angst about how I look is a kind of small-scale moral panic. Calling my brain-farts out of the shadows and up onto the stand for questioning helps with that.

It's also helpful to think of the inverse; *what if I wasn't ugly? What if I was the polar opposite of ugly? What if I was the hottest person on earth?*

Sure, that might be fun for a day, but for most functions of your life, you likely only need one or two or three people to find you attractive. If your face were a universal siren call, how would you get anything done? Wouldn't life be a

constant stream of staring and interruptions and suspicion?
How would you be able to tell who really liked you and who
just wanted people to see you on their arm? The whole
world finding you attractive is a frightening thing.
It's why celebrities live behind high walls and need
bodyguards built like brick shithouses. Is it a life of high
walls you want? Us 'normal-looking' people live free-range
lives, with a manageable amount of perfection, being
recognised for whatever we actually do, not how we look.
What a weird kind of bliss that is, once you think about it.

SELF-LOVE IS NOT A PERFORMANCE, YOU HAVE NOTHING TO PROVE

This won't apply across the board; I know lots of people have
found a beautiful kind of empowerment in showing their body
in public, and what a beautiful, radical act that is. That isn't a
universal experience, but a wonderful one all the same!

But those of us who have spent a lot of energy trying not to be
distracted or self-conscious in public when we have certain parts
of our body on show are often prescribed exposure therapy:
wear the bikini! Embrace the bodycon! Pull on the hot pants!

Sometimes faking it until you make it and putting yourself in
uncomfortable positions in order to build confidence-muscle
is great; but sometimes, for me, it doesn't work. In the end, I
not only feel the discomfort of showing more of my body
than I was ready to, but the added layer of shame having
'failed' at body confidence. *What a poor, brainwashed bad
feminist* my brain mutters under its breath.

This might sound like a Very Silly Revelation to some but: YOU ARE ALLOWED TO COVER UP. Just wear the overshirt, or the hat, or the longer shorts. It's not a big deal. It's not a tragic failure on a grand scale. It's just your body, and as much as you don't need to be afraid of it, you also don't *need* to parade it. You don't owe anyone that.

Gentle encouragement is good, but it seems counter-intuitive to force ourselves to show parts of our body when we're not ready, or comfortable, or when we know it will ruin our day, JUST to prove that we're a good feminist/body-positive ally/kick-ass human, rather than for reasons of real self-embodiment. Sometimes I think there is a pragmatic weighing up to be done between the amount of energy we will lose from *trying* to be someone we are not (yet), versus better uses for that energy. I have found that that brain space often is better spent elsewhere. Sometimes, it's okay to let yourself half-arse self-acceptance.

The area that I struggle with, and I know is woefully common, is my upper arms. Sometimes I can get past the brainfart and take them out on the town, no sleeves; and other days it will just consume my thoughts. For some people, 'letting the thoughts win' would be covering up; for others, it's more empowering to cut your losses and do whatever you need to do to cut the crap and get on with your day. Whilst not entirely half-arsed, another approach for me has been getting really wonderful tattoos on them. I'm proud to show off the artwork chiseled onto the arms I once feared. Now I'm reluctant to put them away! It's a fab feeling to want to celebrate the fact that I *have arms*, and that they're mine and they move, by decorating them; whilst also

having the added benefit of knowing the most noticeable
thing about my arm is now the cool leopard it has on it,
rather than its size or fat percentage.

HALF-ARSE PLEASURE IN YOURSELF

'The pleasure activist', adrienne maree brown, has five
'principles of pleasure' in their book, *Pleasure Activism*.
These are designed to help us navigate the politics of feeling
good, and the last of them has stuck with me the most: that
'the deepest pleasure comes from riding the line between
commitment and detachment'. . . something that they feel
can be applied to anything from work to sex. If that's not
half-arsing, I don't know what is! I particularly love this
when I think about it in relation to our bodies. There's no
greater deterrent to pleasure than pressure. Instead
of fixating on an explosive love affair with our bodies that
might never come, we give what we have to the care of our
bodies, but also know when to step back and know when to
give our appearance a healthy SHRUG. brown is right, there
is a delicious pleasure in edging or flirting with our need for
self-validation. Just enough to ground us in what is,
ultimately, a very cool piece of machinery; but not SO much
that we forget to look around us at all the more interesting
things hanging in the balance.

Right, now we've given our real homes and our bodily
homes a good once over with the 'can I be arsed?' duster, it's
time to crack open the door and take a gander at the world
outside. Shall we pop to the shops?

Half-Arse Hope

A VERY BORING REVOLUTION

My local supermarket was built on the presumption that most people would visit by car. I am willing to bet that yours probably was too. It means that the people who built it made a groovy little plan for *exactly* where they would like you to enter the car park and where to exit after you're done. Of course, they also built a path for pedestrians, with just one entrance/exit on one side of the building.

Slight problem: the pedestrians who live near me can't be tamed. When the hangry hits, we ignore the commands of the concrete and stomp in from all directions. Since they built the supermarket in the middle of a housing estate, with possible shoppers on all sides, they probably should have guessed that there's no way we can be persuaded to walk three sides of a rectangle just to use the 'proper' path. But perhaps the town planner has never craved Hobnobs in the visceral way I have.

The thousands of lawless rerouted trips my fellow citizens and I have made to this supermarket have left their mark. Clear makeshift 'paths' have formed in the grass where we've all cut corners in pursuit of stock cubes, gin, cigarettes and Curly Wurlys. Grass has ceased to grow there, the soil has sunken in, it has become, to all intents and purposes, a path. No one built it. No one planned it. No one can claim to have started it. And yet, there it is, existing, usable, useful, a part of the landscape. These conspiratorial trails have appeared around every supermarket I've ever lived near, but it wasn't until recently that I realised they had a name – several names, actually:

> *Desire Line*
> > *Fishermen's Track*
> > > *Buffalo Trace*
> > > > *Bootleg Trail*
> > > > > *Social Route,*
> > > > > > *Use Path . . .*

Whatever they are, I kind of adore them. They're like a collective conspiracy against town planners, a visual divide in the soil that shows the exact distance between what we expect people will do, and what, in reality, we actually do. If you google 'desire path' or similar, you can see thousands of pictures from all over the world of community-carved paths, veering dramatically away from the pavements and paths laid out for them. Perhaps I'm just strapped for places to find hope, but this silent, undiscussed rebellion gives me a little smirk every time I see one. The desire paths are cooked up by groups of people who are united only by location and defiance, who have probably never spoken and perhaps wouldn't like each other if they did, who don't arrange to meet or agree on a plan but slowly chip away at the default settings of life until they've carved out their own route; what is cooler than that?!

I have also realised that these trails are a great example of how I see 'half-arsing'. To a town planner, or the building firm who spent hours laying and levelling the concrete routes, these makeshift paths might seem like a visual symbol of laziness. They might roll their eyes as anyone might when they spend a lot of money and time on a plan, and the people it was intended for refuse to join in.

But if we look at these routes as Wikipedia does, as 'desire lines', we can see that they're actually secret stompings of real intention. They say: *This is my place, my soil too, this is how I want to travel from A to B, my time is precious and your route doesn't hold any advantage for me. I am prepared to get my boots muddy for a faster route to the crumpets.* They're not only a personal twos-up to what is expected, but collective evidence that low-effort small rebellions can be scuffed out of stubborn soil.

If we start to see the shortcomings and procrastination in our life not as failures, but as 'desire lines', we can start to trace what actually matters to us. If we have never bothered to paint that drab grey hallway and it's been years, perhaps it's time to stop berating ourselves about it. Perhaps whenever you look at that drab staircase, instead of seeing all the ways in which you have failed to express yourself through home decor, you can think of all the things you've chosen to do instead; all the wonderful things you've been swept up in. Perhaps you've been teaching your children the sound of spaceships ripping through the sky, or your rescue cat to trust again, or yourself how to spend less time indoors. Perhaps you've been carving out a career pivot for yourself, or leaving the house to fall in love, or simply just spent that time on the sofa healing your brain. Just because you don't have evidence that can be held up like a trophy in the air, or complimented as visitors take off their shoes, doesn't make those things any less valuable than painting a wall. In this analogy, 'The Wall' can stand in for any of those things that you *feel* embarrassed for not mastering, but are actually inconsequential in the grand scheme of things. They are the shortcuts you have taken in your life because your desire lines got straight to the point, no fussing with the official path.

The more of us that tread these half-arse routes, the more of us will feel allowed to do the same. I've stopped explaining away the state of my house when people visit, because I've realised it sets a precedent for them doing the same when they visit me. Who can be arsed with that? The same can be applied to all the other pointless apologies I have spent decades churning out: *sorry about my hair, sorry about my dietary requirements, sorry about not texting back within ten minutes, sorry to keep 'going on' about that thing I've been struggling with, sorry about the mismatched mugs, sorry about the skin, the work, the existing.*

Once we stop trying to whole-arse the whole of life, and stop apologising for it, imagine the through routes we can create for real progression. Imagine how much space there could be for better stuff. Imagine how much *faster we can get to the crumpets.*

In those times I've felt hopeless, I think I've been waiting for hope to be allocated to me. As if it might be pushed through my door in the form of a leaflet, or published in the form of a graph, or light up my phone with some life-changing green alert from the powers that be. Sometimes I've felt like a failure if I don't have hope, that I should get around to finding it, that once I've found some evidence for it, I can start my life. Hope sure is a slippery thing to get a hold of, but the good news is 'catching hope' is another thing you can strike off your to-do list. You see, becoming hopeful isn't an extra task you need to complete; it's a by-product of action.

It's possible that you've already started to move towards what you want without knowing it. The great hope historian, Rebecca Solnit, says that when asked, we might say that we live in a 'capitalist society' whilst not realising that often the reality of our everyday lives is anything but. Anything we do on principle, for love and for free, is in essence anti-capitalist or at least non-capitalist. From neighbourly favours and community groups to friendships and family lives, our instincts drive us into accidental rebellion at every turn. Our bones know what is important, even before our brains do.

When you picked up this book, you made a move away from the things that you know are distracting you and towards the things you have a hunch are really important.

You're already in it, baby!

If you're trying to be nicer to yourself, you already are. Because you're already *trying*, which is a pretty nice gesture. Get it? If you're trying to clear your mental desk of all the tasks that are diverting you, with a glimmer in your mind's eye of what you would do with that time, you're *already* flirting with a better future. Every page turn is a fluttered lash in the direction of being *arsed* to change everything.

I worry that we're also waiting for 'one solution' that will make us go 'yes! This is worth it! I'll pitch in now!'

Just like in our own lives, there's usually not a magic spell or a tub of cream or a miracle morning routine that will solve it all. Whether you're looking to change the world or just yourself, a 'win' is made up of a lot of little half-arse attempts that add up to the whole; a lot of staggered shortcuts to the supermarket that will create a way forward without us even realising.

We often characterise people who are hopeful as childlike or gullible, but to be hopeful is anything but; it's seeing that, logically, as long as something is *possible*, it's got the potential to be probable. All of the good news stories or inspiring people I've read about came about because someone thought 'screw it, this could work, I've budgeted for the resources we'll need, let's take a whack at it.'

We are encouraged to equate cynicism with being 'smart', but it's often a fear that makes us opt out of giving things a go. I never met a truly cynical person who was also useful. And what's the point in being clever if you're not going to use those brains? Sounds like a very *foolish* smart person to me. The Bulgarian writer Maria Popova puts it much more eloquently: 'critical thinking without hope is cynicism, but hope without critical thinking is naivety.'

Let's get budgeting . . .

HOPE ON A BUDGET

We're all on a budget, what's your limit? Time? Energy?
Money? Now, hopefully in the previous chapters we've
clawed back some of those things for you, but there is, no
doubt, less in the jar than you'd like. But that doesn't mean
it's not enough to have a big impact. Let's deep-clean some
misconceptions you might have about how useful you can be
with the arse-nal you have left . . .

THE SANITY OF SMALL ACTIONS

We've discussed in previous chapters the extent to which
there is any point in you faffing about the individual actions
you can take in your life to 'make the world a better place'.
Largely, the world can't be steered by one person's reusable
cup or eating habits, which is both deeply upsetting and also
a relief. Imagine having that kind of power! Imagine
failing to live up to it?!

That doesn't mean, however, that there's no point in taking
those actions. I like making small lifestyle changes after
finding out new information because:

1. It pisses me off.

No, I'm not someone who gets some kind of sick enjoyment
out of being angry – but attempting to do 'the right thing' is
the fastest way to discover what the systemic issues are
around why something has gone so wrong. If you've ever
tried to book an ethical holiday, buy a pair of fairtrade

knickers or pick up a vegan birthday cake outside of a big city, you might already have glimpsed the struggle. Those lessons are super useful *because* they're specific to my circumstances, and therefore most likely to be within my circle of influence to change. See our chat about 'whole arsing' coming up . . .

2. It makes me feel calm.

It's a contradiction I know, but both things can be true. When I learn new information and don't act on it at all, or at least explore the idea of changing what I do/eat/wear, I feel as though I'm gaslighting myself. As if I want to pull the wool over my own eyes and pretend I never read it. By trying to take even small steps to make things better, I'm at least letting my subconscious know that it didn't imagine the problem, and it also allows me to keep believing that I'm someone who isn't *completely* numb to reality. Throwing your hands up and sighing 'well, what can you do?!' isn't the Zen-master move you think it is.

Knowing that you have a certain level of what they call 'moral consistency' is calming, even in small ways. Being consistent doesn't mean an objectively harm-free, spotless ethical life. What it does mean is that you know in yourself that you're doing what is logistically possible *for you*. I also know that a lot of things I can voluntarily implement today (fewer new clothes, less meat, more time away from screens, a pledge to move my body more) are things that might be necessities in the future. It makes me feel calm to know I'm adjusting early, that the future doesn't feel so full of shocks and radical lifestyle changes. I hear that 'stopping pretending' is the first step in most processes, whether you're healing, grieving, leaving or letting go. Pretending, I reckon, is more effort for me anyway. It takes up huge amounts of emotional energy and time. Stopping that nonsense is a truly half-arsed power move.

3. I'm willing to cough on everyone.

A lot of the 'hopeful actions' we're encouraged to perform can feel pointless, in the grand scale of the problems in the world. And on some level, they are. They're not catch-all solutions, they won't make a big difference, and we shouldn't pretend like they do. In his book *The Tipping Point*, Malcolm Gladwell talks about the misdirected slander directed towards shortcuts when people criticise an action as a 'Band-Aid solution'. He points out that the kind of solution they're referring to is often the most convenient, versatile and inexpensive – and therefore something we're more likely to reach for. Of course there might, in theory, be better solutions, but given the choice between a 'Band-Aid solution' and nothing at all, slapping a plaster on first isn't always a bad thing. Band-Aids allow people to keep working, playing tennis, walking or cooking when, without it, they would have had to pack in their activity entirely. After all, you don't whip out a plaster because you're trying to stop a 'global bleeding crisis'. You whip it out because someone near you has a cut, and you have a quick, painless solution.

We know the half-arsing solution is effective, for good or for ill, because the whole planet has recently experienced its full effects. Geometric progression is a mathematical explanation for how small numbers can escalate into large ones through a series of small multiplications. Each multiplication might seem like it is happening in small increments, but the 'snowball effect' of their growth is huge. The same happened with the pandemic that began in 2020. Only one person needed to sneeze, and it only needed some of that sneeze cloud to land on someone else who was about to board a plane . . . and before you know it we're all locked indoors for years of our lives with only our sourdough starters and our dwindling sense of self for company. None of the *individual* particles of that virus were working on overdrive; there weren't a few girlboss go-getters who were doing more than the rest. As far as we know, there wasn't one 'super-spreader' person who alone infected everyone. No *one* cough did it all, they were mostly very mediocre ones, half-coughs, perhaps half-covered by a hand. The cause can feel out of proportion to the effect, but it happens all the time.

Your small actions don't *have* to be futile. Like we discussed in the chapter on veganism, it's not the strictness with which you follow protocol that makes a difference, but how CHATTY you are about your changes. You spending all weekend indoors, alone, trying to strip your life of all plastic, isn't going to do anything. Sweating the small stuff and trying to be perfect ultimately results in diminishing returns. Making your actions infectious by talking about them and making them easier to copy by changing the systems around you, is what turns them from superstitious rituals into real half-arse strategies.

THE ADVANTAGE OF BEING RUBBISH

The 'Overton window' describes the range of beliefs that aren't your own right now, but that you'd be willing to consider. It is usually discussed in reference to government policies, and how experts think the public will respond to a particular idea, but I think it's a super helpful framework to use in a personal context. In the middle of that range sit the things you definitely believe. Then, a little further out, there's the things you can see *why* people believe, but they're not really something you believe in enough to action, or would be willing to defend. Then, outside of the window, there's the ones that are a little kooky, a little radical . . . and, lastly, your enemy's beliefs – the unimaginably silly, strange or cruel.

In my experience, one of the problems with activism spaces is that they're full of people who have always felt the way they've felt, or who changed their beliefs/habits so long ago that they no longer REMEMBER what was confusing about them, or what persuaded them in the first place. They struggle to accept people who are half-arsing it. Which is unfortunate because, in my experience, most people have time for the people within their Overton window – those that sit either side of them. Like it or not, that's where minds are changed.

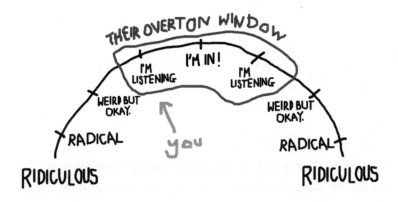

I call this your 'half-arse advantage'. Someone (like you) who has recently shifted their actions or opinions, is much more approachable to the cautious, much more relatable to the resistant, much less intimidating to the wary. A person making a 180-degree turn around in their beliefs is, of course, a wonderful story, but I've found that these instances are rare. Their experience makes a great anecdote, book or movie, but realistically it takes more than ninety minutes to fall in love, more than 300 pages to drop a habit, more than one example to switch a mindset. In advertising, they work on the principle that a potential customer will need to see a product around seven times before they're likely to open their wallet. A lot of people who want to 'change hearts and minds' live as though this transformation can be brought about by one speech, one documentary, one telling off. I've realised that it's much more beautiful and boring than that, and it's done with the necessary humility of someone who has been, up until recently, just like you. If you're cautious about getting in the water, the person you approach first is the one with one toe in, not the person who is already out at sea.

If you've recently changed your mind about something, you have a superpower: you know that you are not your opinions; that shifting your perspective doesn't need to come at the cost of your sense of self. When people hear new information that doesn't align with what they've been taught, I think what they're most afraid of is themselves. They're afraid of who they will be without that part of themselves that they will have to give up, if they listen to the evidence. A half-arse pal is the perfect salve for hurt pride. You can be there to show them all the ways you fail, and the occasional ways you win.

The idea that you are what you believe is a silly one, if not a bit dangerous. If you think that you can't isolate an ideology from a person, it gives you the licence to destroy, isolate, exclude or even kill someone in order to 'get rid' of an ideology. Which, as anyone who has even half-snoozed through a history lesson can tell you, doesn't work. Half-arsers aren't people we should be shrugging through the side doors of campaigns, they should be at the heart of them! They haven't, and won't, work without us!

SIMPLE HALF-ARSE HOPE STRATEGIES

So, instead of a list of tasks, here are some ways you can reframe hope in your mind whilst only having to lift *half* a finger . . .

A DATE WITH YOUR MP

Depending on whether your own political persuasion matches that of your MP, or if your MP is particularly dishy, this might or might not be appealing to you. (Of course, please don't actually ask your parliamentary representatives on a date. Quite apart from propriety, boundaries and what not; we're kind of in a bit of a spot right now, globally – the last thing the rest of us need is you distracting the people in power with your suave charm and good looks. Eyes on the prize.)

A recent *Guardian* survey of the world's leading climate experts ranked voting for political candidates that advocate for strong climate action as the most effective thing you can do as a citizen to help the planet right now – more so than reducing your meat consumption, flying less, improving your household insulation and even having one fewer child.

Seventy-five per cent of people in the UK don't know who their MP is. Of the people who do, can you imagine how many write to them? Regularly? In the gaps between elections, reading their inbox is one of the only ways a member of Parliament can gauge whether they're in favour with the constituents, or if they need to start pulling their finger out. I used to think writing to my MP was a bit pointless. I didn't believe they would write back; I certainly didn't believe they would grant what I asked. If my MP did not agree with what I suggested, or could not be persuaded by my half-baked argument, what was the point? But it turns out that those emails have a greater purpose: data. Each MP's office collects data about the issues that are lighting up their switchboard, and those issues get fed back to the MP in question every week. One email might not make a big impression, but a weekly email? Especially from a number of people? Talking about the same issues? Now, that's graph-nudging stuff.

Anyone who has been a parent, or the very persuasive child of a weary parent, knows that it's not always a tantrum that is most effective when it comes to a child getting something that they want; it's the slow grind that wears parents down. It takes weeks of pestering, of waiting for them to be at their most tired, of turning up regularly to barter for your cause.

A small, well-placed whinge, delivered at regular intervals is what breaks the poor parents in the end.

The same is true when it comes to politics. To move the dial, you don't need a large percentage of the whole constituency to be kicking off about something, you just need to be on the same side as a decent percentage of those who are *writing in*. Which is often very small. If a large percentage of the emails an MP receives are about one particular issue, do you really think that that MP is NOT going to put that issue on their agenda, even sceptically, when they're up for re-election? Or are they going to start thinking 'shit, I better have something to show for myself when I door-knock', however half-arsed and imperfect?

Unlike one-off e-campaigns generated by charities with templates and auto-send buttons, the emails that can really make the impact are the personalised, tailored, consistent ones. The ones that directly link your issue to things that are happening in your area. The ones that include local knowledge and have simple, direct asks.

Even if your MP isn't politically aligned with you and they disagree with the substance of your request, they are still *obliged* to act on your behalf. They can still put your question to Parliament. They can still write to the relevant minister with your objection. Replying that they don't agree isn't as relevant (or as common) as you think it is. You don't need to worry too much whether or not they are nodding along with you; *technically speaking*, their job is to represent your views in Parliament, not theirs.

Where does this date come in? Well, unbeknownst to him, my MP and I have been having weekly tête-à-têtes for months now. I have a recurring event in my calendar that is simply titled 'date with Mark'. It's ten minutes long, and I'm the only one who needs to turn up. (Almost) every week I write him a short email, usually themed around the climate, linked to my local area. I don't try to sound grandiose or like I've gone to Oxbridge. I keep it simple, to the point, polite. Even if he himself doesn't read it I know that in sending that email I've done more than I would if I'd spent that ten minutes stressing over whether a baked bean tin was clean enough to go into the recycling, or whether I'm remembering to bring my reusable coffee cup every time I go to a café.

Can't spend your life campaigning for what you care about in Parliament? No worries. You're actually employing someone to do that for you. That's already outsourced elsewhere and covered in your taxes. Your half-arse quest, should you choose to accept it, is to simply nag them until they start wholearsing as if their job depends on it. Because, as you will remind them, it does.

The more I've thought about it, the more wondrous it seems to me that 90 per cent of the work of democracy (or our imperfect British approximation of it) had been done for me, at great cost, by people I will never meet. They fought for my right to vote (which I wouldn't have had as little as two generations ago; my grandmother was born into a Britain where it was illegal), went to the mat for a health service that made sure I would survive long enough to make good use of it, yelled until I could live in a world where I

241

would be paid enough to have a laptop and an Internet connection through which I can send, at any time, to a member of Parliament, assigned directly to me, a message that will arrive within seconds. Now, that's some wholearsing results right there.

So, make that date work for you. Schedule it for your lunch break, or for over breakfast. Skive a house chore to do it. Miss a week. Only turn up every other time. Blackmail yourself with the promise of a biscuit at the end of it. Take yourself out for a cream tea as a reward. Habit-stack it with your weekly bin day or your laundry wash. No-one minds how silly your system is! If the frequency with which you currently contact your MP is aligned with the world average (zero), then *any* kind of arsing is a huge improvement, and a raised glass to all those who fought for your right to whinge like a motherfucker. To righteously whinge on behalf of others, to whinge on behalf of yourself, to whinge until the floor is no longer made of lava, but of sure footing.

MATCH THE MISSION WITH THE ACTION

Sometimes there's a ropey connection between what we want to achieve, and the action we take that we think will get it done. We can get caught up in the inconvenience or seemingly unfeasible execution of that action, and end up throwing our hands in the air: 'it's impossible!'

I fell into this trap some years ago when someone asked me why, if I was so worried about the planet, did I continue to buy makeup products that were packaged in plastic? *Good point*, I thought. I fell into an Internet hole of research. I tried a whole host of different plastic-free mascaras, reusable packaging, and homemade alternatives. Sometimes it was fun, but mainly it was time-consuming, imperfect and expensive.

Eventually, I threw my hands up in exhaustion and reverted to purchasing the same mascara I had used before, thick plastic tube and all. Not only was I back at square one, but square one tasted a little bit like shame and smelt like despair. A few months later, adorned in my shame-scara, I was reading about plastic waste and fish farming. You might have heard of the 'great Pacific garbage patch', you know, the big lump of plastic in the ocean that can be seen from space? Did you know that most of it isn't made up of our plastic straws and coffee cups and lipstick tubes? No, 86 per cent of all the macroplastics (the biggest, chunkiest pieces) were DISCARDED FISH NETS. Yup. It turns out that 42,000 tonnes of 'ghost gear' makes our little 'stop littering' posters feel pretty flimsy, let alone my little flap about plastic makeup packaging.

Not only had I completely misunderstood what the problem really was, but I'd exhausted myself into apathy before I had even made a dent in it. Mascara, of course, is something I realistically buy twice a year, at most. Fish was something I was eating about twice a week. Moreover, food in general, being something I regularly had to buy because of the whole having a human body thing, would have been the obvious place to start if I was worried about plastic. I was literally buying food in plastic packaging *every day*. So, I stopped eating fish as much, eventually giving up entirely. I started buying individual loose apples in the supermarket instead of in big plastic bags (which also stopped me overestimating my apple consumption and buying too many, only to let them rot). When I could, I popped to a zero-waste shop in the next town over to fill up on what I could afford to fill up on.

I know that I'm not going to single-handedly stop Big Plastic, but I was at least achieving what my silly brain wanted when it started researching zero waste makeup, and then some.

I think my blunder follows a pattern that's incredibly easy to fall into: someone points out something we might be doing 'wrong' and we immediately scrabble to rectify that specific thing.

We don't stop to wonder what exactly it is we're trying to achieve, and whether our efforts might be better spent elsewhere. Most of us don't have time to wholeheartedly tackle every problem, so we need to make that half-arse count.

Essentially it boils down to 'work smarter, not harder'. You'll have ample examples from your own life once you start digging, I'm sure, but here are a few to start you off . . .

1.

Harder Action: Overhaul your wardrobe to be 100 per cent sustainably sourced

Mission beneath the action: You're worried about the impact of fast fashion and landfill

Smarter Action: Start a conversation that goes beyond your own wardrobe

We know that the most sustainable clothing is the stuff you already own, so unless your wardrobe is empty, working with the stuff in your possession right now is the best thing you can do. Don't worry too much about scouring the Internet for the perfect organic t-shirt or hemp underwear, unless you're replacing something that has genuinely gone kaput. If you'd like to put that energy for transformation somewhere, a great place to throw it is into addressing a problem that will impact more than your own individual actions. For example, did you know that 25 per cent of all of the waste clothing shipped to markets like Kantamanto in Ghana are FREE t-shirts? Or for a conventional cotton tote bag to match the same overall environmental impact of your standard supermarket plastic bag, you'd need to use it over 7,000 times (every day for about 19 years).

We're needlessly creating low-quality clothes and bags with wild abandon, often to give away at a one-off event, and it's happening at a scale we perhaps would never guess from our vantage point. If you have any connections with a local charity, or organisation, or company who are in the habit of printing hundreds of t-shirts or tote bags for single events or anniversaries, see if you can get creative and help them think of a better solution. Maybe it's patches that people can iron onto something they already have, something edible in the brand's colours, or, perhaps, if someone is organising a charity run you could agree to simply all wear the same colour, rather than a poorly made slogan t-shirt that would be worn once and then discarded.

You could also organise a local clothes swap in the backroom of a pub, or a charity shop crawl in your hometown, or throw a mending sleepover at your house so you and your friends can all get around to finally darning your socks in front of *Mamma Mia*, surrounded by doughnuts.

2.
Harder Action: Sign up for an expensive gym membership that will motivate you to get fit
Mission beneath the action: You're concerned about your overall health and want to make movement a habit that sticks

Smarter Action: Download some addictive audiobooks or podcasts that you're only allowed to listen to whilst moving

Blackmailing your psyche doesn't have to be expensive. I understand the impulse to shell out in an attempt to leverage guilt in order to get you out of the door, but I know something much more powerful than guilt: an unsolved murder. Holly Jackson is my poison, but you can pick your own. And remember from our body chat; it doesn't matter *how* you move, just that you do.

3.

Harder Action: Have one fewer child
Mission beneath the action: You're worried about your carbon impact
Smarter Action: Move your pension

We simply don't have time to go into it all here, but the carbon impact of a future child is pretty impossible to calculate. Most projections are based on historical data, i.e. the average of what we have used per person in the past; a rate that will be improbable or even impossible in the future. The carbon 'budget' that could potentially be spent on everyone having as many children as they like, is currently being spent ten-fold by inefficient energy systems and the over-production of livestock. (To give you an idea, if we continue on our current trajectory, by 2050 we'll have 120 million more tonnes of extra humans on planet earth, but 400 million more tonnes of extra farm animals to support them. Human reproduction shouldn't be our biggest concern right now.)

Instead of focusing on the hypotheticals, why not try to deal with something that is happening right now? It's likely that, as we speak, your real pension is being used in the real world to fund the kind of future you're a bit worried about future generations having to humour. Most funds invest trillions in fossil fuel extraction, and a portion of that investment is yours. So, instead of fretting about the kind of gas-guzzling car your grandchild might drive in 2078, shift where your money is being invested now. There's a whole host of material online to help you choose a more sustainable pension. The best part about this one is it's a 'set and forget' solution – it will be doing good for you in the background for years to come – you just need to be arsed to set it on the right path once, and then you'll not have to be arsed about it ever again.

4.
Harder Action: Give up all meat in an attempt to be more sustainable
Mission beneath the action: You're worried about the impact of your meals
Smarter Action: Eat chicken instead of cheese

If your focus right now is sustainability and not animal welfare, then you'll have a much greater impact, and maybe have to make much smaller incremental tweaks to your meals, by cutting out (or cutting down your consumption of) cheese, beef, lamb and prawns rather than becoming an all-out vegetarian straight away. Cheese creates three and a half times more greenhouse gas emissions than chicken. The same goes for coffee versus farmed fish; contrary to what you might expect, coffee production produces just over three times more emissions than fish. So, if impact not labels is what matters to you, having one less cup of coffee a day, or swapping your cheese sandwich for an egg one, still makes a big dent in your individual resource use. Of course, it's just the beginning (I can see a delicious chickpea sandwich in your future!) but if the thought of hopping to a completely different diet is daunting, try some easy swaps before pulling all meat from your menu.

5.
Harder Action: Giving up chocolate for Lent
Mission beneath the action: You want to have better impulse control/you're worried about your eating habits
Smarter Action: Spend forty days getting curious about why you feel like that

This one is usually born of a worry that we are overconsuming something, or that our mental restraint is low. Instead of wiping chocolate from the menu completely, which transforms it into the forbidden fruit that now looks twice as delicious and drains us of mental energy as we spend all of our powers of restraint trying to resist it, try to use Lent as an excuse to finally get to the root of the cause. Half-arse it by booking in ten minutes a day into your calendar to journal/read about why you might have problems with impulse control and pledge to have an action plan by the end of Lent. Or perhaps, instead of taking chocolate off the table, promise to try one new snack a day: one of them might become the staple you reach for in future.

MAKE A SMALL ACTION INFECTIOUS

As we've discussed, the critics are right. Small actions aren't *nothing*, but a little bit of contagious behaviour can turn a *titchy* little change into a rippling big wave. Take a small change that you have mastered and make it your *Mastermind* topic of choice. Maybe you're the composting queen of your clan, but you know one compost heap does not make a revolution. Become the geek of the group, make it your go-to tipsy rant. Learn to build compost boxes and share what you're doing on your social media – not with the tone of 'you should be doing this too, naughty naughty!' but in the spirit of 'look at my weird new project, isn't it gross and cool?'. Offer to collect your circle's compostables if they can't do it themselves. Find out what's stopping them and don't berate them, complain to your council about the roadblocks that are holding them back.

Keep at it, in little low-effort ways. Grow houseplants with the fruits of your compost and gift them to friends. Make it known that you're the pal to call should anyone have any composting queries. Write a 'can you compost this?' pub quiz round for your Christmas party.

If you're trying to be a half-arse vegan, send your experiments (fails included) to the group chat. Make your default party offering delicious and (p.s. surprise!) vegan. Batch-cook and offer some to weary friends when they're having a hard week. Be the person to research the restaurants with the good vegan options. Let them know you're open to questions, admit when you don't know, admit that you have a Curly Wurly on special occasions. See if anyone wants to join you in campaigning for Cadbury's to make them vegan.

Maybe you're the re-use royalty of your group. You gift refillable toiletries as birthday gifts. You bring multiple reusable cups to a meet-up, you offer them up casually without pressure to accept. You email your group's favourite brunch spot to ask if they might switch to using ketchup bottles instead of sachets.

I am attempting to be the slow-fashion nerd amongst my friends. I willingly offer up my wardrobe for borrowing requests, I put out asks for scrap fabric on my close friend stories on Instagram, I've thrown swap parties and take our hang-out walking routes past charity shops. I am willing to be the 'what do you think about this brand?' designated chat bot, even if my friends could research it themselves. I make myself available to teach small sewing tricks or to hem jeans. I get geeky about fabric types and wear my self-made items to parties and always make sure to compliment people when I recognise an item they keep wearing:

I always love seeing you in that top, remember the last time you wore that and we went to that pub and we laughed so hard Guinness came out of my nose?? It reminds me of that day, I love it when you wear it!

Omg is that the same dress as the one you wore to that gig? It looks so different and new the way you've styled it.

A PROBLEM SHARED IS A PROBLEM HALF-ARSED

If you have found true friends within a twenty-minute walk of where you have eventually settled in your life, please write a book about how you did that because I would like to know.

As I mentioned, I have been (so far) unsuccessful in persuading my 'village' of friends I made in the first three decades of my life to move near to where I have finally 'settled down'. The stats reassure me that I'm not alone. In the UK, only 21 per cent of the population say they *never* feel lonely; everyone else rates themselves on a pretty alarming sliding scale of loneliness, with the most lonely being those under thirty-five. It's likely that wherever you live it's not looking much better, since the World Health Organisation recently declared loneliness a 'pressing global health threat'.

The causes are too broad to tackle here and too varied to solve with one solution, but far from giving up, I'm here to argue for the perks of half a loaf. Why? Because without a *bit* of company we can't even begin to start feeling hopeful. That might sound like a sentimental statement, but it's much more of a biological one.

We've heard the old adage about people's periods syncing when they live together (seems like science hasn't gotten around to properly exploring this, but I can tell you from the anecdotal evidence of my life: *totally* true) . . . BUT have you heard about all the other weird ways our bodies sync up with each other?

If you watch a piece of live theatre with other people, regardless of whether you know them or not, your heartbeats can synchronise. Temperature contagion is the phenomenon of your body temperature altering in empathy with others. Researchers found that when participants watched videos of people plunging themselves into cold water, their own body temperature dropped to correspond with what the stranger was experiencing. Susan Pinker is a developmental psychologist who has published some fascinating research on the biological necessities of face-to-face contact. It seems that, no matter your personality or natural inclinations, a life with little in-person social interaction can be medically dangerous; in real terms, it can be as bad for you as smoking a pack of cigarettes a day. Our physical resilience is influenced by the quality of our social interactions; from colds to cancer, the people most likely to recover have a strong, physical social network. The benefits include the way that interactions can affect the body, like reducing hypertension, or the fact that if you're seeing people regularly, you're more likely to mention health ailments to friends and receive encouragement to get them seen to.

Since so much of our communication is non-verbal, it makes sense that digital interaction doesn't have the same effect. According to Dr Albert Mehrabian, who specialises in psychology at the University of California, only 7 per cent of our communication is verbal, with 38 per cent of it being tone of voice and 55 per cent being body language. And, in a fast-changing technological revolution where we're disengaging from physical interactions at every turn – whether that's online shopping, QR-code-ordering in restaurants, or remote meetings at work – when exactly are we supposed to practise our fluency in these unspoken languages?

I can see evidence within my own life of this. It's not just the form the communication takes, but the longevity of an in-person interaction compared to a digital one. For starters, a face-to-face interaction is much more effort to arrange;

there are people that I interact with casually online without thinking too much about, but would I brush my hair and catch a bus to have that same interaction? Most of the time, probably not. So, if I meet up with a friend in person, I've already invested in it in a way that social media can't rival. It's no guarantee, but while I'm with the person, we're much more likely to have a more meaningful exchange. It's often been that over text or even voice notes, I'm able to brush off the signs that I'm having a rough time with an 'I'm fine'. In person, where my mood is harder to hide, my response is harder to edit and, in general, I'm exposed to their soothing company for longer, I can relent and share how I'm *really* doing. I can't walk away if they pull me up on something I've said, or ask me a question that challenges me.

Interestingly, acting on Pinker's research doesn't necessitate making lots of lifelong bosom buddies. The 'weak ties' of Meg Jay's research (that we discussed in the vegan chapter) show up again as the research demonstrates that these weak ties can be equally as valuable as having an intimate circle. Social integration on a general level ties with close relationships as a predictor for how long you will live, even when the research is controlled for mitigating factors. These types of integration scored twice as high as clean air, exercise and quitting alcohol as indicators of your general health outcomes.

This doesn't mean becoming an extroverted party animal or the supercharged scout leader of your friendship group overnight; the benefits are incremental, just like any other lifestyle change. As we discussed in the body admin chapter, the impossibility of you becoming a gym rat or an athlete doesn't detract from the benefits of an occasional jog around the block. Half-arsing is allowed.

Social neuroscience as a field of study isn't much more than two decades old, so, given the span of human existence, we presumably have a lot more to uncover. But what has already been established stands up truthfully against thousands of years of anthropological evidence. It's worth looking into yourself, as the research is fascinating, but the top line is: *online interaction isn't enough!* We need to get our arses out of our seats and to the pub, or the park, or the draughty village hall.

Does all of this research add up to some lofty, hackneyed advice about putting away your phone and touching grass? Not so fast . . . in fact, far from exacerbating our problems, I think that utilising our digital circles might be the key to solving our loneliness epidemic, we've just got to be open to some half-arse connection.

HOW TO MAKE SOCIAL MEDIA MORE SOCIABLE WITHOUT REALLY TRYING

Perhaps I have a vested interest in defending the online space as it's where I work, love and learn. On the other hand, perhaps that makes me more qualified to say that, contrary to popular belief, the Internet is as much of a 'real' space as any, in the ways I think 'real' should be qualified: full of real people, with real feelings, looking for real interactions. It might not have a loo or a kettle, but the online spaces I have found myself in as an adult have been as functionally social as any draughty church hall or nightclub I've attended 'in real life'. Sometimes more so.

It's easy to forget that your connections online aren't cyborgs or avatars, but lovely three-dimensional people who have sniffles, gestures and backs of heads. So, here's some small steps to use social media to strengthen your connections rather than string them out . . .

Look at your ratios!

Regularly look through your most-DM'd people and ask yourself when the last time you SAW them was, or if you'd trust them with a big problem. I can fall into spending my time online interacting with the people who will respond the fastest, or who are also posting a lot – but they're not necessarily the people I miss, or really want to connect with. The availability bias of it all! I try to rebalance that either by asking the people I've been DMing out for a drink (no shame in being blunt: 'I'm trying to get better at actually SEEING all the cool people I chat with on here, so: 'Thursday, cuppa?') OR using the time I would have spent DMing people via apps to actually text the people I haven't heard from in a while.

Post your point of view

If you feel like you've been trained to think of social media as a way to frame yourself and a way to control the way people see YOU, try flipping that on its head. Your social media accounts are a place to show the world how you see IT. You can reach out and swing the spotlight around.

What's the view like from where you are? What are the best things you spot in your day? What can seem mundane to us can offer others wonderful little glimpses into the small parts of a life that make up the whole. I love seeing my long-distance friends' favourite plants, the weird meals concocted by my extended family and views from the windows of new acquaintances. The best posts are very much 'half-arsed', not curated within an inch of their life, and not overthought.

The Internet is also a great place to share new things you're learning about, or your ideas for ways the world might change, without accidentally being directly confrontational with the people you love. It's hard to bring up world events or complicated injustices in casual conversation, but when I've posted about these topics on my social media feeds, it's been a 'way in' for people I see regularly in real life to bring up subjects we would have never discussed otherwise. It's a way of me sharing (as we discussed in the vegan chapter) that I'm not sure about chopping up and eating something that has hobbies, or that I'm open to chatting about my thoughts on trans rights, without directing those thoughts at anyone in particular, or making my loved ones feel like I'm 'finger-pointing'.

So, what does the world look like TO YOU? You
can take this literally, and make the decision to only post pictures FROM your viewpoint, never of yourself; or you can interpret it as a metaphor and start asking 'what do I want this to show people?' before you click 'post'. As a guide, I try to make sure I'm using the camera on the back of my phone as often as (if not much MORE than) I'm using the selfie camera at the front.

Say it out aloud

If you're messaging someone, keep in mind that research about non-verbal communication. Consider communicating in a video or voice note rather than a text-only reply. It can feel much more spontaneous and I find I'm able to reply more consistently as I'm not faced by a daunting blank text box. There's also a level of intimacy to how troll-like I will allow myself to appear in video calls to close friends. It's a humbling but held experience to be seen at your *least* washed and still be listened to. I've received everything from little videos of charity shop hauls to fifteen-minute book review rants from friends, and each time it's made me feel special and thought of, however random the topic.

Never send a meme alone

Recently I've tried to practise something I'm tentatively calling 'intentional meme sharing', which is as pretentious as it sounds. Arguably necessary though, as I fear that some of my interactions with friends are solely made up of us sharing short-form comical videos with each other in the hopes that, hours later when the recipient sees it, it will make them chuckle. This habit has a very pure motive, but I'm also trying to remember how addictive these apps are designed to be, and how incessant. A phone that would otherwise remain untouched buzzes with a silly meme sent by someone with an equally dark sense of humour/intense interest in the subject of the meme, and before I know it I'm forty minutes deep into a scroll hole I would otherwise have never gone near. My solution is to save up a few funny posts to send all at once, perhaps when we're already chatting. Or, if I just want to send a single post, I make sure I'm sending a line of text or something that says why it specifically reminds me of them, or why I thought they'd like it. Something that strengthens the connection as much as it makes them chuckle.

Make social local

The strength of the 'weak ties' that Meg Jay talks about are stumbled on most easily nowadays via your phone. If you feel as though social media is making you more disconnected from the world on your doorstep, never fear – your doorstep *also* has social media. We're much more likely to be fed posts from big nationwide or global-appeal pages, but really the most magical part of my social-media-socialising has come from 'local social'; making a conscious effort to start mapping out my links to my immediate community, through my feed. That means following local small businesses, social enterprises and community groups. You don't have to engage straight away, be a local lurker. It's a great way to get a sense of what might be going on beyond your screen, and what you might be able to join in on. I've been introduced by mutual friends to people in my area over direct message, I've kept in touch with local artists I've met at craft fairs, I've offered to take up the jeans of local business owners who ask for help on their stories, I've popped in to local book events, I even asked my brother's celebrant for a coffee after she officiated his wedding and I realised she lived locally . . . thanks to social media! Following someone on Instagram can feel a lot less abrasive than asking for someone's number, and is a great way to browse through all the things you could have in common, especially if they've been following my first tip and using their feed to show the world from their point of view.

It's up to you to curate your feed, it's definitely not what the bots and the algorithms want you to use it for, but I really believe, if we use it wisely, it's still one of the best tools we've got to connect in real life.

GET SOME FRIENDSHIP RITUALS

I've gone from wincing at the sound of the word 'ritual', as something enforced and whiffing of religion, to wondering whether my friendships are *made* out of rituals; those repeated patterns that we build meaning out of. In Alain de Botton's *Religion for Atheists*, he suggests that 'we have allowed religion to claim as its exclusive dominion areas of experience which should rightly belong to all mankind' – which is, in my mind, a fancy way of saying: 'your friendships are cults, lean in to it.'

From the meals we eat to the times of year we meet, to the strange nicknames we have each other saved as in our phones, good friendships *should look weird* to an outsider. They should need explaining, they should require backstory. Some of the rituals I have with my friends bear no relevance to the point of this book, but a few that I think fall into the category of 'half-arse' are as follows:

1. We have a rule that we're not allowed to leave before putting the next meeting (or phone call) in the diary, allowing us to not have to be arsed later about

remembering to arrange the next meet-up or spending weeks exchanging possible dates before giving up.

2. We write agendas of things we'd like to cover when we see each other: it's a fun way to make sure everyone gets a turn in a group, and also to make sure I open up about something I might otherwise, in the moment, want to bottle up.

3. Staying in touch doesn't have to be a big task. In between meeting up we keep our communication quick, easy but tangible: quick snaps of mundane moments, short voice notes whilst walking to the supermarket. I even have a stack of pre-addressed postcards to my friend Rah that sit on my desk, and whenever I have a moment I write her a three-line note and pop it in the post.

THREE IS NOT A CROWD

Some of my strongest friendships are trinities. One triad was formed as a teenager, when, at the age of fourteen, one of my childhood best friends from around the corner introduced me to her 'new best friend'. A surge of jealousy was immediately followed by a rush of affection that has lasted two decades and counting. Although we do meet up one on one, our default mode is to wait until we can hunker down with a bottle of wine as the 'complete set'. The other is with two women I met through the Internet, at the same time as we all became 'creative freelancers'. In lieu of colleagues and appraisals, we have formed a 'business club' that meets every quarter and lasts all day. Think *Macbeth* witches, but with MacBooks instead of cauldrons.

I should have guessed that strong friendships come in threes . . . PowerPuff Girls, Stooges, Amigos, Musketeers and Bee Gees . . . but the half-arse benefits were not intentional. And yet, on reflection it seems to be the secret sauce that keeps us together, especially when our resources are limited. It means you don't have to hit every mark as The Perfect Friend, but the hurly burly still very much gets done.

If someone is having a late-night meltdown, *one* of us is likely to be up, even if the other is fast asleep. If someone is grieving, *one* of us will know what to say. There are two pairs of eyes to spot if one of us is flagging but won't admit it, two brains to solve a logistical riddle, two diaries to help us remember a birthday. When you have a problem to workshop, there are two perspectives to pick from or mix together. When you need to go off grid for a bit to birth a baby or a big job opportunity or a book (let's say), you're not leaving your friend in the lurch: they can tag-team with your trio's other member until you're back on track. It's honestly one of the parts of friendship that makes me understand polyamory; when you always have backup, it's more likely that everyone's needs will be met.

Jeffrey Hall, professor of Communications Studies at the University of Kansas, has categorised our expectations for friendship into six categories: genuine positive regard, self-disclosure, instrumental aid, similarity, enjoyment and agency. That's a lot, and meeting all of them sounds daunting. *Meeting half?* Doable! In her brilliant article for the *Atlantic*, 'Stop Firing Your Friends', Olga Khazan suggests that rather than expecting a few close friends to fulfil all of our needs, a healthier approach would be to see friendship as a crowd-surfing experience, depending on a wave of hands to hold us up.

The dials of my friendships have been turned up or down over the years, depending on what we're going through, and how much time we have, or who is best placed to support someone. A group approach, even if it's adding just one more person to the mix, means that we can be excused from the table to half-arse things when we need to, whilst knowing that our adored mates will get spotted while we're sorting our shit out.

UPSKILLING OVER FINDING BEST FRIENDS

Put 'friend' into a thesaurus and the synonyms you're given are active. *Accomplice, collaborator, aide, deputy, supporter, helper, accessory, companion, comrade, colleague, crony.* The requirement isn't so much 'being' a friend, but 'doing' a friendship. A friend isn't necessarily someone you are identical to, or who compliments your personality in every way. They're someone you *get stuff done* with.

I love this idea of friendship needing a subject matter, of forming as you look towards something else, not so intensely at each other. Looking back at the catalysts for most of my friendships, I've often met them in the 'third spaces' we spoke about in the chapter on finding a sense of home. Instead of spending hours hunting down a perfect 'making friends' strategy, the half-arse approach is to make sure you're turning up to those third spaces that would be 'typical' for you. The kinds of places those who love you might go, 'Oh, you saw Leena there? Well, that's typical.' While I'm yet to form those 'close bonds' locally, I've already met wonderful people in my area by simply lingering like a bad smell in all those places that 'of course I would be in'. This, for me, an avid nerd, means chatting to the woman with the great handmade jumper in my local bookshop, turning up to local writing workshops, showing my face regularly at my local pub quiz.

There's a lot of truth in the old adage about romance being something that 'strikes as soon as you stop looking for it'. Similarly, I think stopping trying so hard might be the key to accidentally finding real friendship. And, as we know the floor is made of lava, it's great to start building practical connections with the people around us, of all ages. *If* we are looking at a future with fewer readily available resources and a more local approach to food, work and mending, it's time to start getting used to working with the people around you, and focusing on upskilling our communities while it still feels like a fun choice and not a necessity!

From growing food to mending clothes, cooking to first aid, what are some basic skills you are lacking – or, even better, think you can pass on? If we only have limited time and energy to devote to things outside of our work or home commitments, picking a practical activity over a purely social one can help to get us out of our own heads. It puts less pressure on making instant connections and even if we don't get a friend out of it, at least we have the little duck we've learned to whittle out of a tree stump, eh?

HOPE, ANYWAY

When people ask me about hope, I hear an echo of my childhood self turning to a parent; '*is it going to be okay?*'. Maybe I should be embarrassed to admit this, but now, in my thirties, I often turn to my partner in those moments when I'm struggling to articulate what I'm worried about and ask instead; 'is it going to be okay?'. He, depending on the situation, will give me one of the following:

A) an affirmative 'Yes! Of course!'
B) a truthful 'I don't know, but I'll be here either way', followed by a hug.
C) a heavily sarcastic 'NO, IT'S ALL GOING TO BE TERRIBLE, MIGHT AS WELL QUIT WHILE YOU'RE AHEAD AND GET OUT NOW!' and I am forced to laugh: at myself, at him, at the world.

Whatever his reply, asking the question aloud and voicing it to someone else has a soothing effect. I've realised that behind so many of my anxieties, whether it's about myself or the world around me, is the secret belief that it's possible to *know*. That somewhere there is a huge switchboard of factors, running the odds through a control centre, assessing my chances. That if only I could get in there, if only I could crack the code, I'd be able to see. To see whether it's worth trying, if my half-arse makes half a difference, if I should give up before I've even begun. If such a place did exist, I imagine there would be a long line of people outside, all wanting to be told straight:

Am I going to be able to change? Am I capable of this? Will it work? Will my kids be okay? Will my life always be like this? Will things be different? Am I doing enough? Being enough? Saying enough?

It's only by making peace with what we will never have, that we can enjoy what we do. I don't have a magic portal through which to peek at the future, but what I do have is the past and the present. The past shows me that the world is capable of radical change. The present shows me that it is already happening, and at a rapid pace. We shouldn't be kept from doing what we can, simply because it isn't what we imagine to be 'enough'. We shouldn't relegate ourselves from living a good life, just because it's not a perfect one.

At the end of the day, humans have a long history of gambling. We rub sticks together even though we've never seen a flame before. We pick and eat strange-looking plants that could fill us up or kill us. We wander into the next valley even though the one we grew up in is fine. We still get married even though we're constantly reminded that these partnerships have a 50/50 chance of failing*. We love to throw our chips in and cling to the chance that the dice will favour us. Even if you're not feeling factually optimistic, given the odds, you'd be carrying on a long human tradition of throwing your chips in anyway, jumping and trusting the air to catch you.

*Fun fact; that number is now down to 29.5 per cent in the UK — either we're getting better at picking partners, or we're not marrying the wrong person to begin with! Hurrah.

What to Whole-Arse

I'm afraid this next bit is up to you. True to my word, I'm tapping out with the job half done. Like I said in our first chat, this book is not about half-arsing absolutely *everything* in your life, but clearing your to-do list of 'things to perfect' so that there's space for one or two things you can be *really* effective at.

So, now that you've cleared up all that space in your brain and your calendar, what should you do? What should you focus on?

You might already have a good idea of what you want to give your 'whole arse' to: perhaps it's writing a novel, or climbing every Munro mountain in Scotland, or *finally* finding a career that suits you. Maybe someone needs your whole self right now: you're raising a mini human to be a happy adult, you're accompanying someone through the last era of their life, you've got a relationship that needs some serious TLC.

Perhaps you started this book without a clue and then became distressed/enraged/galvanised during one of the chapters as I suggested you half-arse something you *definitely*, now you think about it, want to whole-arse!

Fabulous! Crack on! You're dismissed from the table, feel free to close the book and go and throw yourself into that thing that is worth everything you've got.

But, if you're still at sea, if you're still looking for what deserves all your can-be-arsed energy, here are my suggestions . . .

THE ANSWER IS ON YOUR NOSE

Advice that attempts to have universal application, whether that's on 'how to change the world' or how to 'change your life', often appears in a diluted form that *everyone* (in theory, if not in practice) can replicate . . .

Sleep more, fly less, drink more water, recycle your soup cans, eat less meat, buy 'this' many items of clothing, buy reusable coffee cups, reduce your plastic use, have one less child, eat your five a day, take ice baths, do mindful journaling, practice face yoga.

This is the magic number, *the* magic formula, *the* magic ingredient.

That *feels* very warm and fuzzy but it's a total red herring when it comes to effectiveness. Whether you want to bring about a shift in the way your town, your city or your country runs, or you just want to make some headway with improving yourself, the best thing you can do is often the thing that *only you can do*. The more specific you get, the more effective you can be. Want a graph to prove it? Here you go . . .

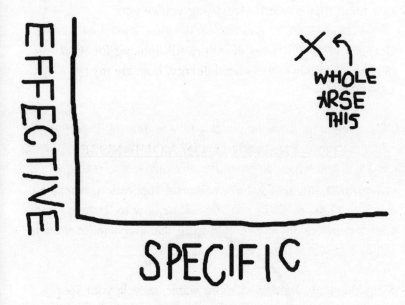

If you're a glasses-wearer like me, you've definitely had an occasion, in a time of extreme exhaustion or tipsiness, when you've bellowed:

I CAN'T FIND MY GLASSES!!!

And, after a long pause, someone else in the room has rolled their eyes and said something to the effect of:

You're wearing them.

Often, we imagine that the answers we're seeking are something alien, unknown, that we have to turn out the drawers of our life or traverse the globe trying to find them.

More often than not, they're on our nose. So close we'd forgotten that they were there.

What is on your nose, then? Without a crystal ball or the powers of omnipresence, how can I help you work it out? Hands up, I probably can't – BUT I know someone who can.

The presenters from the podcast *How to Save A Planet* suggest drawing this diagram and filling it in with the specifics of who you are, and what you have. It's an exercise that really changed my mindset for the better, so let's do it together.

WHAT ARE YOU GOOD AT?

This can be very literal; what field did you train in? What industry are you already a part of? If you already have sway in your workplace or your field, you'll have much more impact there than spending all your energy trying to edge your way into another one in your spare time or trying to cram making change into your out-of-work hours. Whether you're changing a policy or the way a department works, starting a union or pushing for more veggie options in the canteen, if you're working from the inside of an organisation you'll pack much more punch and likely upgrade your colleagues' lives in the process. (Sidenote: doing a self-starter side project that is change-focused as part of your job also looks great on a CV. Not the point, but a very welcome byproduct.) Industry-wise, you'll know better than an outsider how a system works, where the gaps are, and what could be better. Maybe the answer is embedding yourself in a system in order to tweak it and nudge it in a better direction, or maybe it's setting up your own thing and rewriting the rules about how your skill can be put to use in the world.

It can also be broader: what communities are you already a part of? What is something you don't mind doing that a lot of people avoid? What's your *Mastermind* topic of choice?

WHAT IS THE WORK THAT NEEDS DOING?

You can load any social media feed or crank open any local paper to find what the problems are. Spotting the gaps is down to your skilful eye. Maybe the world needs more 'third spaces', like we talked about in the home chapter, or easier ways to have a 'mushroom wardrobe', as we discussed in the chapter on personal style. Better trains, better politicians, better restaurants, better plumbing, better social services, better roads, better cookie recipes, better social media platforms, better working hours, better pubs. There's not a thing in this world that couldn't do with an upgrade, so I'm going to leave this one to you.

WHAT BRINGS YOU JOY?

For me, the more joy, the less drainage in my soul. There are secret reserves of energy and enthusiasm tucked SOMEWHERE inside of me, that somehow my body will only let me access if I do the fun thing. Fun doesn't have to be the easy thing, or the dancey-prancy thing, or the childlike thing. It can be the puzzle that needs solving, the case that needs cracking, the enduring persistence involved in sending *yet another* chaser email to your MP to remind him to get his arse in gear. Look at any online fandom or chronically niche local club to see how humans flock to the minutiae; applying almost manic persistence and taking pleasure in the details most of us would find infuriating.

It's also great if this list is a list of things you think you could keep up long term; perhaps you've worked on something similar in the past, or have evidence from your life that you're likely to stay interested in that activity.

Now you've got lots of ideas in each circle, which things could sit in more than one? Is there any through thread or project that might incorporate all three? Whether you're into

video games or vintage cars, you're a Brownie leader or you
do parkour, ask yourself: what could make this community
better? Last longer? Include more people? How can we be
more ambitious with what we're trying to do, and/or more
focused on what's possible if we put our heads together?
What about a Taylor Swift group that goes to climate
marches together, or a vintage car event that also educates
people on the future of travel? A parkour group that
advocates for better town planning, or a Brownie pack that
holds workshops to teach the grownups how to bake vegan?

Doing this exercise actually led me to start my podcast, *No
Books on a Dead Planet* (the tagline: we read climate books,
so you don't have to!). I'd already run a few podcasts as part
of my various jobs in marketing, and also in my free time. I
owned some basic podcasting equipment. I adore chatting
about books, and know a fair bit about the kinds of books
that are out there. Something that a lot of people avoid but
for some reason doesn't faze me is public speaking.
Something I think the world needs is more access points for
talking about the climate crisis. There are lots of serious
books on the topic and lots of documentaries to watch, but
as well-meaning and worried as I was, I avoided reading
about the climate crisis and struggled to have conversations
with the people in my life about it. That seemed to me to be
a big problem with the climate movement: we had solutions,
we had plans, but very few people were crossing the
threshold that took them from mildly interested to keen and
ready to tackle stuff. Like any hard topic, it's so much easier
to talk about once you've overheard other people talking
about it, and without talking, you can't start doing.

So, the podcast is a way to give people the opportunity to eavesdrop on an imperfect, chatty climate conversation, between non-experts who just want to get over their fear of looking the problem in the face and (where possible) having a little giggle too.

Draw the circles, have a think, see what pops out.

HALF-ARSE EXPERIMENTS

Still not sure how to fill in those circles? Let's scale things back and run some low-effort, short-term experiments to see what we can unearth . . . starting with re-phrasing the questions:

~~WHAT ARE YOU GOOD AT?~~ WHAT ARE YOU CLOSE TO?

Remember when we talked about the tipping point? Instead of thinking of 'good at' as a specific skill, think of it as your unique position in the world. Perhaps you've built up a good relationship with your place of worship and you're well known there. You are the favourite grandchild to a grandparent who will listen to reason from no one else. You live in a place that has been forgotten in some way, or misunderstood. You have lost a parent, a grandparent or child and have all this extra love and energy to give, with nowhere for it to go. Perhaps you are trans, or living in a disabled body, or from a specific cultural background that most of the general public don't really 'get'. If you're not sure, spend a few weeks with the question in the back of your mind, and write down every time you have an experience you don't think everyone does, or you talk to someone who doesn't speak to people often, or you notice something about where you live that could be better.

At the end of the experiment you'll have a long list of possible leads to pop in your empty circle – you might even have to rub it out and draw a bigger one!

~~WHAT IS THE WORK THAT NEEDS DOING?~~ WHAT'S STOPPING PEOPLE?

Look at the advice around any of the topics we've discussed in the book: self-sufficiency, confidence, style, getting moving, advocating for yourself at work . . . and think about what is stopping people from doing those things. If there was a moment while you were reading where you thought *'Leena, this is such an unrealistic suggestion! Loads of people couldn't follow that advice because of _____'*, then that '_____' might be where you begin.

~~WHAT BRINGS YOU JOY?~~ WHAT COULD YOU KEEP DOING FOR A LONG PERIOD OF TIME WITHOUT THROWING IN THE TOWEL?

'Joy' often conjures the wrong image; it's not always giggles and rainbows when it comes to a calling. It can feel hard or tedious while you're doing it, but after a day of getting on with it you feel a sense of vigour and completeness. Like you became more resilient for having got through it, like you could get better at it if you rinsed and repeated. I'm not one for 'airy-fairy' language, but I have experienced that feeling of 'being in the right place' or 'being in my element'. Don't kick me for saying this, but sometimes it just 'feels right'.

Try to list some moments in your life where you might have felt like that, however small or seemingly insignificant. What kinds of skills were you using? What kind of environment were you in? They're all clues in the mystery of you, so keep sniffing until you unearth a bone.

THOROUGHLY PLANNED; NEVER EXECUTED

I adore planning things; I spend hours on Tripadvisor, bookmarking hostels or little cottages on far-off cliffs and in distant towns. I have a digital board pinned with patterned fabric and silhouettes and sleeve patterns for a dream wardrobe. I have at least seven folders of podcast concepts that I know would be stonkers, if I could only get them off the ground. I've mapped out whole novels, including character profiles and sketches of their office floorplans. Once I even planned a whole conference, including when the cake breaks would be and which workshops would run when, led by dream workshop leaders I neither knew nor knew how to contact.

Another essential part of my hobby of planning things is telling my friends. I'll paint them elaborate verbal pictures of the bookshop-come-event-space-come-teashop I will open, the literary walking tour company I will start, the satirical political party I will found. This habit has pluses and minuses. I get the thrill of sharing my new whacky plan, but am also haunted by them, years later, when a friend reminds me of a plan I never followed through on, especially if that moment coincides with me launching into news of a new fizzy, thrilling idea.

The audacity of their attentiveness! How dare they. If I believed I'd get around to it, I'd put 'get new friends' on my to-do list.

In my meaner moments, I am exhausted with myself. All the time I've pitted away, mapping skies I never actually fly through, tracing blueprints I'll never build. Is it all pointless, I wondered?

And so, once, I tried to give up the pointless planning. I resolved to only spend time thinking and taking notes on something if I was ACTUALLY going to do it. And do you know what? It was miserable. My mind was either bored or found other, self-distructive ways of entertaining itself. And some days, it was impossible. Even with the 'omnipresence' of screens, the tick-tick-tickering of an idea would plod around after me, prodding me for attention.

Then I read a 2010 study of 1,530 Dutch adults, where they found that their participants' highest levels of happiness occurred in the lead-up to a holiday. This elevated mood might be experienced for weeks or even months before they left. Once they returned from the trip their levels of happiness dropped back to around the same level as those who didn't go on a trip at all. In fact, people who travel frequently were shown in one study to *only be 7 per cent* happier than those who didn't do any travel. From arena concerts to weddings, big trips to baby showers, you can find forums of people who are gathering, confused, to wonder why the event they had planned so elaborately, and which went so smoothly, made them feel nothing.

Rather than take this as a lesson in how reality is always a bummer, I think there's something very useful to learn about the benefits of letting yourself plan without judgement. How it might have a value in itself – regardless of whether you get around to the execution, regardless of whether you 'can be arsed' to finish.

I have a suspicion that so many of us who feel shame for having 'poor follow-through' as adults were fantasists in childhood. We were the ones who didn't just make their Barbies kiss, but invented whole social hierarchies within, and generational drama between, their sets of Sylvanian Families. Deprived of the dollhouse, we moved on to spreadsheets, Post-it notes and Pinterest boards.

I realised that I wasn't failing at finishing. **Starting things was** *part* **of my process.** It was a way of whittling ideas down, giving each one a little air, a little water, seeing which would burrow furiously down into the earth and stop me from sleeping, and wilt in daylight.

Being a fantasist is the stage before being a realist. Not the kind of cynical realist who accepts how things are and rolls their eyes at those who won't, but the kind of realist who creates reality, assembling it from hidden clues they can see that others miss; who spots change coming over the hill whilst the rest of us are looking down at our to-do lists.

We're often encouraged to judge ourselves based on the ratio of plans we make to those we follow through on. To be someone who does everything they think about doing is to be a 'go-getter'. I've come to disagree – the higher our ratio of ideas to things we actually do, the better the things we actually choose to do will be. We've considered all the options, we've made peace with what we did not choose, and we've made sure that what we do follow through on is the best option possible.

All of this to say, give yourself time to get stuck into this exercise. Do it several times over. Let yourself guess and mess around and fill pages with pointless pondering. Half-make a plan and then start again. No one finds the answer without a lot of crumpled paper around their ankles.

BUMS ON SEATS

Picking 'a thing' can be scary, and I think it's because we believe that to pick 'a thing' is to turn our backs on all of the other things. If we pick this artistic medium, does it mean that we're never going to be allowed to dip our toe in another? If we choose to go to the wall against fast fashion, does that mean that we can't care about famine, or breast cancer, or endangered giraffe breeds?

Those who pick 'a thing' are often heckled online for *all* the things they did not pick. *You speak on X but what about Y, your silence on X is noted, your efforts only solve this issue but what about that one?*

I agree that in some instances, doing absolutely nothing is *weird*, and failing to recognise the interconnectedness of issues can make for some sloppily executed change. However, the people who remain hushed and unheckled are the ones who pick *nothing*. We relish the opportunity to take the active people down a peg, even at the risk of humiliating them back into doing nothing.

That's why I think that the world might run a little more smoothly if we were all permitted one cause to truly focus on, to get geeky about, to deeply understand and start to tinker with. Then build a half-arse strategy for the rest.

Author and campaigner John Green tells the story of his work with Partners In Health, a non-profit focused on social justice in the health-care sector. He points out that often, when we see a disaster on the news, we give our money and attention without deeply engaging with the root cause of the problem, and as a result often end up supporting short-term interventions that either do very little or don't strengthen systems in the long run. It also gives us a warped idea of problems in the world 'never' being solved, as we let our attention shift as the news cycle does, never lingering long enough to really listen or to witness improvements after the fact. There is always another earthquake, another flood, another war to watch on our screens. In 2014, John contacted Partners In Health to see what they were going to do about the recent outbreak of Ebola in Sierra Leone, and if he could help.

His contact explained that, since 15 per cent of Sierra Leone's healthcare workers had already died of Ebola, it would be even more catastrophic if charities came in, offered some support and then left. The Sierra Leonean healthcare system would be left in an even more precarious state than it was to begin with. 'So, we're going, but we're also staying. And we want to ask you to stay too.'

And so Green pledged to remain involved, to listen and make his attention open-ended. As a result, he's been a big part of a new maternal hospital being built in the region to not only tackle maternal and infant mortality (1 in 20 women in Sierra Leone has a lifetime risk of death related to pregnancy or childbirth, which is among the highest rate in the world), but train new local medical professionals. Staying so the next catastrophe will be less catastrophic is his suggestion, and it sounds sensible, doesn't it?

What we need, essentially, is to sit our arses down. To be ready to remain seated through the whole thing, not lingering at the door, occasionally poking our noses in and then wandering away. The 'stay' game plan needs bums on seats, not musical chairs.

Where do we get all this time, though? To sit, to listen deeply, to work out the best strategy for fixing an issue, getting to know all the key players, the mechanisms and the true needs. For John Green, it would seem it comes from a place of making peace with having picked. And the equally vital part: not expecting the same of others. He builds strategies that require some half-arse actions from his large online community: small, quick commitments of time, money and attention.

If your 'whole-arse' isn't a personal challenge but one that you'd like to ripple out further, remember that it will probably be most effective if the strategy depends on a small group of people wholearsing for the cause, and the majority of people participating in it only ever committing a small amount of time or money.

Perhaps create your 'asks' around time increments: if you only have five minutes, do X, if you have thirty, do Y, if you have one day a month, come and join in with Z.

Equally, if your 'whole-arse' is something personal that requires the attention of others – perhaps you want them to attend a show you're putting on, or read a regular newsletter, or understand the wonders of a franchise you love – then it's also worth taking their half-arsing into account. How can you summarise it for them? How can you make it easy to interact or join in?

80,000 Hours is a non-profit organisation who help people choose careers that have the largest possible positive social impact. While they're all about finding people jobs that make a big impact, even they admit that in some cases, it might be better for people who (for admittedly unfair reasons) can sell their time at a high price to forgo volunteering and instead earn money that can be used to fund a cause (provided of course that their job role doesn't actively conflict with said cause – an oil strategy adviser working overtime to donate to Greenpeace would be at best ironic and at worst would be taking the cause one step forwards, two steps back). An example that springs to mind is ClientEarth. They're an environmental charity made up of highly skilled international lawyers who have only one client: Earth. They sue people on behalf of Earth. Of course I want more laws to change, and legislation to be put in place to protect the planet. HOWEVER, I was agog when I learned how many laws and bits of legislation are already in place, ones that people have already fought tooth and nail for, but simply aren't being adhered to by governments and companies.

I want what they want, but I know that their aim requires a high level of expertise in the field of law. I also know that I'm no Elle Woods, my time most probably would be of very little use to them. So, to honour the people who have already sacrificed so much to create the laws, who have already whole-arsed it, my half-arsed support is to give a monthly donation to them to simply sue the arseholes who don't adhere to the laws that protect the planet. It doesn't feel as flashy or as wholesome as some other kinds of charity, but it's honestly a strategy that I believe will work.

In the event that you can't, or aren't ready to, choose a whole-arse pursuit but want to make a difference, you could instead make a list of three artists, organisations or campaigns that are really going for it in a way that you respect, that impress you, that give you hope. Look for their half-arse 'asks' and try to fulfil them when you can. The role of Arse-Enabler is yours for the taking, we need you.

Most importantly, we have to be able to recognise that it is not disrespectful or lazy for someone else to half-arse something we see as our 'stay' project. While we should be up on how our focus is interconnected with other issues and factors, we're only going to win if we allow others to focus on what matters to them, just as we are. It's much more efficient for us to trust that others can choose their wholearsing focus for themselves, and use the energy that might have been spent bemoaning their inadequate response elsewhere – perhaps thinking of strategies about how better to engage them, or working out who might be more effective for us to talk to instead.

THE ARSE END OF SOMEWHERE

So there you have it. I'm going to kick your arse out. I've taught you everything I have to teach you, it's just you and your butt now.

I hope you're ready to stop hovering over your seat and plonk yourself down in life, the show is worth seeing and there's a lot to clap about.

As a final reminder that perfect is pointless, I'd like to tell you about the history of the phrase 'pull yourself up by your bootstraps'. To the modern ear it describes the act of going it alone; of achieving greatness without any external help. A person who 'pulls themselves up by their bootstraps' has reason to be proud: they've succeeded without whinging, against the odds, no fannying about.

Except, that's not how it started. The story goes that its first appearance in print was in an American newspaper in 1834, in a sarcastic account of somebody attempting something totally absurd. 'Probably Mr Murphree has succeeded in handing himself over the Cumberland river, or a barn yard fence, by the straps of his boots.'

The phrase is then used throughout the nineteenth century as a way of laughing at those who attempt silly feats, or to criticise governments for expecting the impossible from its citizens rather than helping them. Here's one from the *Vermont Watchman and State Journal* in 1836:

'It is no less preposterous, that a government, whose constitution recognises the rational freedom of its subjects, should hope for perpetuity, with a due encouragement of practical education, than that one should attempt to lift himself up by pulling at his own boot-straps.'

I wonder how much that shift in the way this phrase is used is part of a societal tendency to put all the responsibility for 'winning' on the individual and all the blame on them when they lose. That we *could* be extraordinary is a compliment, but the expectation that we *should* be is a one-way ticket to hell. It's easy to absorb this mindset without realising it, and very hard to shake once it's in there.

Over the course of this book I hope you've been able to laugh at yourself for setting yourself impossible expectations and then berating yourself for not meeting them. Whilst we might be able to do *anything*, it's not fair to expect ourselves to do everything. Not only is it pointless; it's lonely. When you can do it all yourself, there's no excuse to bring other people along for the ride. And, as we've learned, we *need* other people. If half is all you have to give, then that's great news; you have room to be joined by someone else who also has half. That's just maths.

If you feel spent, you're not the only one. Luckily, morsels of energy are still energy, specks of hope are still hope, you never have nothing. I have never personally witnessed a *completely* empty peanut butter jar. Even when someone declares it 'gone', there's always something to scrape and spread across your toast. Besides, how boring it would be to be a finished product, what hell it would be to be whole! To half-arse is human, to arse it up and dance anyway is divine.

You and your arse have a long way to go, but the view from the side of the mountain is still pretty nice. I'll see you there and I'll bring the Curly Wurlys.

Acknowledgements

———

Some thank yous are in order.

To Craig, who makes a mean cup of tea and an even better partner. Without you this book would still be on my pie-in-the-sky-to-do-list. Thank you for always being willing to keep rowing while I hang off the helm singing ditties and forgetting to steer.

To my editor Kate, whose brilliant harebrained ideas have always got me into the best of trouble. To my co-editors Lauren and Josh who now know my deepest darkest secrets (mainly that I can be hypocritically type A when I want to be, but also spell like I'm drunk and treat commas like cheap confetti). To my agent, Hattie, for securing the bag and being lovely about it.

To Rah, George, Kelly, Ariel, Hannah and Lucy, all of whom frog-marched me over the line into writing this book whilst I squealed *'but what if I can't!!!!'* like a wee little kidnapped piggie. You collectively have served one hundred and three years of knowing me. Terrifying! Please let me stay snug in your good graces until we are old.

Acknowledgements

To my beta readers for being nothing short of alpha on all
fronts; Rosianna for deleting every nervous 'I think' and
'perhaps' before statements about which I was actually quite
certain (*SAY IT WITH YOUR CHEST!*); Paddy for
protecting me from my own dark humour; Sara for her
unbridled enthusiasm; Helen for her annotations worthy of
their own stand up show; Sanne for pulling me back from the
brink of my Britishisms; Lex for their eagle eye; and Lily for
generously laughing at my bad jokes.

And, finally, to the not-really-strangers who have met me in
the small pub of the internet to generously swap ideas,
drinks and kind words: please accept this book as my round.

Notes

Further Half-Arse Reading

A hand-picked, abbreviated list of interesting resources I found while writing this book, should you want to explore some of the topics I've discussed.

Choices

The Glass Half Full: How Optimists Get What They Want From Life – and Pessimists Can Too, Suzanne C. Segerstrom, Robinson, 2009

'The Science of Procrastination & ADHD', Sci Guys Podcast #228, 2022

Washing Up is Good for You, Dept. Store for the Mind, Aster, 2017

Personal Style

www.GoodOnYou.eco

'Where Do Your Old Clothes Go?', Lucy Rodgers, BBC News, 11 February 2015, www.bbc.co.uk/news/magazine-30227025

'Clothing Returns Are Killing Us?', Cary Sherburne, Texintel, www.texintel.com/blog/clothing-returns-are-killing-us-did-you-know-that-most-returns-end-up-in-landfill

'Your Brand New Returns End Up in Landfill', Harriet Constable, BBC Earth, www.bbcearth.com/news/your-brand-new-returns-end-up-in-landfill

Consumed: The Need for Collective Change: Colonialism, Climate Change & Consumerism, Aja Barber, Brazen, 2021

Home

'Moving On, a Love Story', Nora Ephron, *New Yorker*, 29 May 2006, www.newyorker.com/magazine/2006/06/05/moving-on-nora-ephron

'I Watched 151 Celebrity House Tours and They're Full of Lies', Kendra Gaylord, YouTube, 2023, www.youtube.com/watch?v=9X8M7ENDlJ8

'Maybe Nancy Meyers Doesn't Want You to Stop Focusing on Her Beautiful Movie Kitchens', Yohana Desta, *Vanity Fair*, 10 June 2019, www.vanityfair.com/hollywood/2019/06/nancy-meyers-movie-kitchens-sexism

'The Housing Crisis is Still Being Underplayed', John Burn-Murdoch, *Financial Times*, 12 January 2024, www.ft.com/content/f21642d8-da2d-4e75-886e-2b7c1645f063

'Which Houseplants Should You Buy to Purify Air? None of them', Sarah Gibbens, *National Geographic*, 14 November

2019, www.nationalgeographic.com/science/article/
houseplants-dont-purify-indoor-air

Losing Eden: Why Our Minds Need the Wild, Lucy Jones,
Allen Lane, 2020

Body

'There's a Way to Get Healthier Without Even Going to a
Gym. It's Called NEAT', Will Stone, NPR, 22 July 2023,
www.npr.org/sections/health-shots/2023/07/22/
1189303227/neat-fitness-non-exercise-activity-thermogenesis

'The 10,000 Steps Myth', Maintenance Phase podcast, 25
April 2023

*How the Body Knows Its Mind: The Surprising Power of the
Physical Environment to Influence How You Think and Feel*,
Sian Beilock, Simon & Schuster, 2015

Pleasure Activism: The Politics of Feeling Good, Adrienne
Maree Brown, AK Press, 2019

'Skin Care: Is Anti-Aging a Scam?', Science Vs podcast, 18
May 2023

'How the Anti-Aging Industry Turns You Into a Customer
for Life', Emily Stewart, *Vox*, 28 July 2022, www.vox.com/
the-goods/2022/7/28/23219258/anti-aging-cream-
expensive-scam

'The Review of Beauty' Substack from Jessica DeFino

Clean: The New Science of Skin and the Beauty of Doing Less, James Hamblin, Bodley Head, 2020

'Your Amazing Regenerating Body', Gaia Vince, *New Scientist*, 14 June 2006

'What Those "Dermatologist Recommended" and "Clinically Proven" Labels on Your Lotions and Soap Actually Mean', Lydia Ramsey Pflanzer, *Business Insider*, 20 October 2015

Work

'Why Women Don't Apply for Jobs Unless They're 100% Qualified', Tara Sophia Mohr, *Harvard Business Review*, 25 August 2014, hbr.org/2014/08/why-women-dont-apply-for-jobs-unless-theyre-100-qualified

Religion for Atheists: A Non-Believer's Guide to the Uses of Religion, Alain de Botton, Hamish Hamilton, 2012

'Stop Firing Your Friends', Olga Khazan, *The Atlantic*, 28 June 2023, www.theatlantic.com/ideas/archive/2023/06/stop-breaking-up-with-friends/674540/

Hope

The Village Effect: Why Face-to-Face Contact Matters, Susan Pinker, Spiegel & Grau, 2014

'Strong Nonverbal Skills Matter Now More Than Ever in This "New Normal"', Jon Michail, Forbes, 24 August 2020, www.forbes.com/councils/forbescoachescouncil/2020/08/24/strong-nonverbal-skills-matter-now-more-than-ever-in-this-new-normal/

On Connection, Kae Tempest, Faber, 2020

'Hope is an Embrace of the Unknown', Rebecca Solnit, *Guardian*, 15 July 2016, www.theguardian.com/books/2016/jul/15/rebecca-solnit-hope-in-the-dark-new-essay-embrace-unknown

'Is Your Carbon Footprint BS?', How To Save a Planet podcast, March 2021

'What Are the Most Powerful Climate Actions You Can Take? The Expert View', Damian Carrington, *Guardian*, 9 May 2024, https://www.theguardian.com/environment/article/2024/may/09/what-are-the-most-powerful-climate-actions-you-can-take

'The Cotton Tote Crisis', Grace Cook, *New York Times*, 24 August 2021, www.nytimes.com/2021/08/24/style/cotton-totes-climate-crisis.html

'You Want to Reduce the Carbon Footprint of Your Food? Focus on What You Eat, Not Whether Your Food is Local', Hannah Ritchie, Our World In Data, January 2020, ourworldindata.org/food-choice-vs-eating-local

'Does Writing to Your MP Actually Work?', Leah Astbury, Amnesty International, 26 January 2017, www.amnesty.org. uk/blogs/ether/does-writing-your-mp-actually-work

Therapy is . . . Magic: An Essential Guide to the Ups, Downs and Life-Changing Experiences of Talking Therapy, Jo Love, Yellow Kite, 2021